Understanding the Impact of Trauma

Identifying Care and Therapeutic Interventions

Pat Frankish

Understanding the Impact of Trauma: Identifying Care and Therapeutic Interventions

Published by:

Pavilion Publishing and Media Ltd
Blue Sky Offices
25 Cecil Pashley Way
Shoreham by Sea
West Sussex
BN43 5FF

Tel: 01273 434 943
Email: info@pavpub.com
Web: www.pavpub.com

Published 2023

A catalogue record for this book is available from the British Library.

ISBN: 978-1-803882-87-1

Pavilion Publishing and Media is a leading publisher of books, training materials and digital content in mental health, social care and allied fields. Pavilion and its imprints offer must-have knowledge and innovative learning solutions underpinned by sound research and professional values.

Author: Pat Frankish
Editor: Mike Benge
Cover design: Emma Dawe, Pavilion Publishing and Media Ltd
Page layout and typesetting: Phil Morash, Pavilion Publishing and Media Ltd
Printing: Independent Publishers Group (IPG)

Acknowledgements

I would like to thank all the people involved in the work that led to this book being written. I include all the individuals whose stories I tell, their families, supporting staff and commissioners of services. It needs a coordinated effort to meet the emotional developmental needs of all of us and anything we can do to facilitate that must be good. Thank you.

Contents

Preface

This book follows on from the successful assessment tool, the *Frankish Assessment of the Impact of Trauma* (FAIT), and could be seen as the next stage in my journey with understanding trauma. It takes the FAIT as a starting point and evaluates how it can be used more widely, capturing the consequences of trauma in the stage of development before a fully-formed self is established and providing guidance for intervention that is proving to be extremely effective. There are lots of stories here about people who have benefited from the use of the tool and the understanding of the impact of trauma. All of the work is underpinned by deep psychological theory of the development of self.

Traditionally, psychoanalysis has been the only way to approach early trauma and this is not readily available or economically viable. Furthermore, it has never been the norm to provide psychoanalysis for people with limited cognitive ability. The FAIT was developed for those who work with people with intellectual disabilities, however some of the later chapters in this book explore the wider use of the tool. It's difficult to talk about incidents from childhood, and there is always a fear that somebody will recognise the individual and their family. Because of this I will vary some of the details in order to ensure anonymity.

The more I have studied the impact of trauma, the more I have come to accept that trauma is part of our everyday life, for all of us. For most of us, it shapes who we become and is not a problem. But for many people, there is a continued issue which becomes problematic. And because the trauma is usually experienced, initially, during the pre-verbal stage of development, and then impacted and exacerbated by further trauma throughout life, it is difficult to understand. This leads to inappropriate treatment, more despair, and significant dysfunction in life.

I have come to the realisation, over time, that the term "emotional disability" is an appropriate term that could be more widely used. With people who have early trauma and cognitive impairment, we find that emotional disability arising from early trauma has a further impact on the person's cognitive ability. As a consequence, for those who have a diagnosis of intellectual disability and complex behaviour problems, the combination of emotional disability from trauma and intellectual disability from a variety of causes leads to a very complex picture. Sadly, many of the people who fall into this category end up in restricted environments because their behaviour is not understood. This is further compounded if their intellectual disability is mild or moderate, as there can be a wholly unreasonable expectation that, if they are less impaired by their intellectual disability, they can or should behave better. But if we consider an individual who is 30 years old physically, perhaps eight years old cognitively, but only 18 months old emotionally, we can see how the complexity can lead to difficult behaviour. However, we do know now, and this will be described throughout the book, that if we address the emotional disability we can provide significant relief from the impact of trauma, and enable people to access more of their cognitive ability.

We are finding that more people are open to thinking about the impact of trauma and its relationship to complex behaviour patterns. After many years of using medical or behavioural approaches, mainly because of the lack of availability of professional staff who can address deeper emotional issues, we have come to the development of the FAIT, which is a straightforward way of assessing and indicating interventions that can be carried out by social care staff, teachers, parents and the full range of health and care staff who may be involved in a person's life. It has been possible, by using this tool, to get away from the mystery of psychoanalysis while at the same time capturing what trauma means and what needs to happen. The crucial factor in all of the interventions that will be described in this book is the availability of the right emotional support provided in the right way at the right time. This sounds very simple, but is not necessarily always easy to achieve. I have found, generally, that staff groups and families immediately identify with the issues once they are pointed out and are positive in their willingness to provide the appropriate intervention.

Having been involved in services for people with intellectual disabilities for most of my life, I think we are reaching a stage at which we are able to provide more humane care for the most distressed group. If we can change the term 'challenging behaviour' to distressed behaviour, we will be making a move in the right direction. If we can support staff to support the individual who is distressed, we will again be making progress. Positive behaviour support (PBS) has become the intervention of choice in disability services and has a lot to offer. However, it still struggles to address the needs of the people who are pre-individuation in their emotional development. It is possible to use the PBS model to describe an intervention that does address the impact of early trauma and it is hoped that this will be further developed in the very near future. The group of people with intellectual disability and emotional disability will always be relatively small, but it is the group that is the most demanding and most expensive to support. It must follow that an approach that can be used by everyone is a good way forward. And even more appropriate is the consideration of early identification of trauma. If all who work with the under-fives were aware of the signs of interrupted emotional development, we would see a significant reduction in the distressed behaviour that I referred to above.

Note on terminology

Looking through history, we find the frequent change of name for the condition of intellectual disability. In the last hundred years or so, we have used terms from mentally deficient and mentally handicapped to learning disability and now to intellectual disability. Similarly, we now refer to mental health rather than mental illness. I have, for the most part, used 'intellectual disability' throughout this book, however there are times where, due to the context, I have used other terms.

It seems that, as a society, we struggle to accept people who are different in some way and find ways to label them. And these labels, over time, become pejorative. There is a need for people to be accepted as people first, with all the little quirks and individualities coming second. The more tolerant we are of difference, the less intolerant we become of people who are frequently struggling to manage in the world they don't understand.

Valerie Sinason has spoken eloquently about this in her book *Mental Handicap and the Human Condition* (1992). We all struggle with difference, and if we could get to a position where we celebrate the fact that we are all unique, and therefore all different, the world might be a better place. And, certainly, people who are presently rejected by society would have more opportunities.

Chapter 1: Introduction

This is the starting point of the whole story, which covers a significant part of my life, and I hope gives you a feel for what is to come. It feels quite momentous to me that a relatively simple way of seeing emotional development can be so complicated.

The story begins in an old, long-stay hospital for people with intellectual disabilities, previously referred to as 'mentally handicapped'. My parents worked in the hospital and we lived in the grounds when I was a child. I later returned to that house as an adult and worked there too. By this time, I had children of my own, and had not yet started my studies in psychology. But even as a child I was struck by the behaviour of some of the distressed people that I saw every day, and I was puzzled. I was also distressed to see people who were clearly unhappy, and staff with limited options for what to do. I saw incidents of people being restrained and injected with tranquilising medications, put into seclusion rooms, and being generally ostracised. At the same time, I also saw lots of fun activities, real attempts to provide quality of life activities, work opportunities, real care in the face of physical illness, and a collective belief that what was being provided was the right thing. I remember the day rooms with coke-burning stoves behind metal guards. I remember the ladies wearing dresses that were almost uniform; pink, green or brown gingham, fully lined with cambric, which chafes under your arms. On a lighter note, some of the metal fire guards later became a cage for my tortoise.

I remember a little boy, probably aged four, on the ward where my mother was the ward sister. He was in a cot all day and night with a net over the top to stop him climbing out. He battered himself most of the time except when asleep and was covered in bruises. Nothing seemed to help him and we were all relieved when he was moved to another hospital. I would see him now as a traumatised child in need of a lot of care and attention. I remember a middle-aged lady who walked around the grounds all the time, often shouting, often stopping to deposit faeces on the floor, with everyone accepting that this was who she was, and not questioning or understanding the meaning of her behaviour. This lady, with the hospital closure programme, moved to social care in the community and her behaviour changed as soon as she was in a different environment. I remember wondering, as well, why there were only adult females and children at this hospital, but no adult males. I was later told that it was policy not to mix adult male and female patients in the same hospital, so as to limit the possibility of sexual liaisons. It also became knowledge to me later that some of the ladies were there simply because they had had a child out of wedlock. It also became known to me that some of the people were detained because they were 'feebleminded', a term that seems quite pejorative but was clearly acceptable at the time. The person with the power seemed to be the consultant psychiatrist, who came one day a week and held case reviews. What he said was always followed; often medication and the clear acceptance of the fact that very little could be done to change the behaviour of the people he was reviewing. (It was always a man in those days, although now more consultant psychiatrists are women.)

This was all within my lifetime, so it was not that long ago that we were following such discriminatory policies.

There was a period in the 1950s and 60s when there was a desperate shortage of nurses, and still a belief that this population needed nurses, and it was at this time that state-enrolled nurses were established in addition to the state-registered nurses. My mother was a state-registered nurse for the 'mentally subnormal', which was another term used at the time of her training. She later received a Jubilee medal for her many years of service to nursing, which I still have. The wards in the hospital where I lived were relatively small compared to some other hospitals. It was a small hospital with 200 beds and six wards, so none of them were very big. The children's wards were small and most of the children were physically disabled as well as learning disabled. They had facilities introduced in the 1970s, after the Education Act, including physiotherapy, occupational therapy, speech therapy and teaching. They had a hydrotherapy pool installed and the quality of life was much improved, although it was still very much institutional care.

When I went to work in the hospital, I began to understand some of the difficulties. My job was to provide daytime activities for the group of 16 adult female patients who were considered too disturbed to go to occupational therapy and stayed all day on the ward. I had no previous experience of a job like this, but I worked out that I needed to know what they could do, what might interest them and what facilities were available. We identified a small room that could be made available. I divided the 16 women into four groups of four. I assessed them individually on three skills: a screwing and unscrewing rod for manual dexterity; a nine-piece jigsaw to see what they could make of that; and pencil and paper to see if they could produce a drawing. What became evident very quickly was that they had more skills than was obvious from their daily behaviour. Over a period of 16 weeks, they had one session a day for each group and in those sessions we did drawing and painting, played games and engaged in social activities.

They seemed to benefit straightaway from being in a smaller group. It also became evident that one lady, who had a diagnosis of manic depression, showed her mood through her paintings. When she was depressed, she painted a whole sheet with black paint, and when manic would use lots of bright colours. All showed themselves able to concentrate and interact in this particular setting.

I also realised two things about myself from this exercise. One was the realisation that I had an ability to work creatively with people who are different. The second was that I might be able to go to university, after I was introduced to the visiting clinical psychologist who showed an interest in my work and encouraged me to study psychology. The benefit for the individuals who engaged in the exercise was a wider appreciation of their ability, and their need for diversionary activities. The results were also taken seriously and the activity sessions were continued after I left,

Although I didn't at this stage have any formal training, it seemed common sense to record some data. This I did from the point of view of skill level. Each lady was assessed at the beginning of the intervention and again at the end. All of them made progress, adding weight to the belief that meaningful activity might be useful. What I didn't understand at that time, but came to understand later, was that one of the factors that influenced the women's engagement and the progress they made was the positive interaction and attention provided by me in the small group sessions. In those days, back in the 1970s, people were beginning to look at behavioural approaches in addition to medication and basic care, but no one was really looking at the emotional needs of this population. I remember the clinical psychologist telling me about the behavioural system, where you give attention to someone doing what they should be doing and remove attention otherwise. This works to some extent with some people but not others, and settled the question in my mind at that time as to why this was the case. It was to be many years before I could explain it in terms of emotional as well as cognitive impairment.

I was fortunate to be offered a place to study psychology at the University of Hull. This was not as easy option with three dependent children, but it proved to be an extremely valuable experience. For my dissertation, I studied the communication needs of a non-verbal child with cerebral palsy and designed a speech synthesiser for her. This utilised the buttons of a calculator and, if she could press one, it would speak a sentence for her. This gave her more freedom and a better quality of life and confirmed for me that my future may lie with people like her.

It was nearly seven years later, after bachelors and masters degrees, that I returned to the same hospital to help with its closure. I had qualified as a clinical psychologist and undertaken a job in the neighbouring authority, which had then taken on responsibility for closing this hospital. I did not expect to be in that situation but, as it happened, what I had learned and what I knew about the individuals was helpful. During my training, I had been given an opportunity to study psychodynamic psychotherapy as well as clinical psychology, and this led me to look more deeply at the meaning of behaviour. During my clinical training I was asked if I could provide individual psychotherapy for a non-verbal child with an intellectual disability. I was apprehensive about engaging in something that was not generally acceptable. However, I agreed, found a supervisor, and offered ten sessions to a little boy. He was a very distressed child, largely out of control and very difficult to help. It was a big surprise to all of us when he immediately responded to the therapeutic space and therapeutic toys that I offered. Within a few sessions he was almost transformed into a less-anxious, more-contented child who was able to accept the help that was offered to him. This included being willing to eat properly, sitting at a table, and to allow people to change him, very quickly leading to him choosing to use the toilet himself.

Then, later, in the process of belonging to a supervision group, I came across Margaret Mahler's book, *The Psychological Birth of the Human Infant* (1979). This was a real lightbulb-moment for me, in that the behaviours that Mahler describes in children in the stages between biological birth and establishing a whole self at age 3½ to 4, were the behaviours I was seeing in the hospitalised population of people with severe intellectual disabilities and complex behaviour. This led me to ask the question, "do these individuals have an emotional developmental delay as well as their cognitive impairment?" Since then, I have gone on to explore this question and researched it in some detail, leading to my doctoral thesis, and from there to the development of the *Frankish Assessment of the Impact of Trauma* (FAIT).

Some of this story has already been told in my book *Disability Psychotherapy*, and here I am going further, to talk about the application of the theory and to argue for its wider use in understanding complex behaviour. We need to understand the impact of trauma in the early years if we are going to be able to identify care and therapeutic interventions. Having used this understanding over some years now (over 40), I have come to accept that much distress could be avoided if we can adopt and put into practice approaches that meet the emotional developmental needs of babies and children (with or without cognitive impairment). It is of great interest to me that the psychoanalysts who were writing in the 20th century had a lot of useful things to say but did not generally manage to make their knowledge widely available. The idea of attending psychoanalysis sessions five times a week does not appeal to many people, and is not generally available because it's too expensive. But Donald Winnicott, John Bowlby, Melanie Klein and others have written extensively and provide us with valuable insights into the development of the sense of self that we all need if we are going to be able to function successfully as adults. Margaret Mahler, with her colleagues Pine and Bergman, was working in America at the same time, and her contribution, for me, is that her theory and description can be made available to a much wider audience than those who can attend for individual therapy. And that has been the driver for my work and is the driver behind this publication now. We have had lots of opportunities to put the theory into practice and this has confirmed the findings of these authors, encouraging me to try to make it more available to more people. The publication of the FAIT has been significant in this work. Training in the use of the FAIT is available and is being accessed more all the time.

What I plan to do throughout this book is to give you some insight into the application of the theory, the usefulness of the FAIT, and some real-life stories that will hopefully bring it alive for you. There is much joy to be had from helping someone get in touch with their emotional self, and even more helping them to recover, develop further, and go on to lead much richer lives. One of the big factors that has always been present in intellectual disability work, apart from constant change of its name, is the belief that the condition of the brain is fixed and immutable. And, of course, physical changes in the brain leading to the intellectual disability can't generally be changed. But the emotional disability that comes from the early trauma which has not been understood at the time, is able to change if the right emotional environment is provided.

The term 'trauma informed care' has, unfortunately, come into regular use and is being misused. Most people can understand trauma from the point of view of road traffic accidents, abuse and cruelty, war and other events involving pain and distress. But when I talk about trauma, I'm talking about events that, from the outside, may have looked perfectly normal, but are not understood by the young child experiencing them, and are therefore traumatising. Sadly, one of the most common traumatic events children experience is the arrival of a sibling. This changes the whole life the child and, mostly, parents recognise that it is traumatic and enable their older child to manage and process this change. But there are other situations where it is not noticed, or, if it is noticed, parents don't know what to do and do not necessarily receive the right support from professionals.

If there is a difference between the older child and the new arrival in terms of disability, it makes the situation immediately more complex. If the older child has a disability, the reaction to the new child may be not as obvious as it would be in a child without disability. A child without a disability can still be traumatised and may show behaviours that indicate this. Most parents find it more difficult to interpret the behaviour of a disabled child. When doing my assessments, I always ask an open question about trauma, using the words, "Can you think of anything that you remember clearly that happened before your child was aged five?" There is always, and I repeat, *always*, a clear memory that comes straightaway, of something that the parent can remember but that was not interpreted as traumatic at the time. These can often be fairly simple events, often associated with the arrival of a sibling, but sometimes a hospitalisation of the mother or the child, accidents in the home or the car, and a whole range of incidents.

One mother told me a story when her son was in his 30s, of a distressing journey home from the seaside when he was 15 months old and had screamed all the way. When she changed his nappy on arriving home, she discovered that his whole nappy area was burnt, and he had clearly had something to drink that didn't agree with him. He was still behaving in his 30s at the emotional age of 15 months, and was obsessed with his bottom area. This obsession was clearly a disadvantage to him in public and he was living in quite a restricted environment as a consequence. Parents and professionals would be unlikely to see that event as something traumatic, and something that might have a life-long impact. But we need to get to a point where we recognise that trauma happens when there is an event that is not understood. And the younger we are, the less we are able to understand. Acknowledging the impact of traumatic events that take place during the critical stages of emotional development between birth and the established sense of self as a separate being, is crucial. Sadly, it's also very painful to accept that little children can be traumatised by what are, to some extent, ordinary events. It is also very positive to realise how many children are resilient and not affected too much by such events. So, there is a balance between where you are and who you are when the event happens, the severity of the event, and the outcome. What is most reassuring is to know that, once identified, the trauma and its impact can be addressed and progress will be made. Most of the work done so far using this approach indicates that the recovery time is approximately the same as the time the developmental stages would take if they progressed naturally. It follows, therefore, that someone stuck at the emotional development stage of a one-year-old stage may need two or three years of planned input to enable them to reach their potential.

Chapter 2: Historical context

This chapter attempts to put the work on emotional development into a historical perspective, exploring how policy changes over the years affect what is accepted and what becomes new policy.

It seems important to put what I'm saying into some historical context, perhaps looking more widely at service provision than what I have considered so far. We need to remember that it's less than 100 years since people with intellectual disabilities were treated as people and not non-people.

I have always admired the work of the trailblazers who brought the needs of people with intellectual disabilities into the mainstream. My professor at my first university, Professor Alan Clarke, was influential in changing the way that people were seen. At the time of his seminal work, the term 'mental deficiency' was used in this country, and 'mental retardation' in America. Prof Clarke, along with A A Baumeister in America were among those who engaged in detailed research and were the first to show that people with limited cognitive skills could learn. Before that, it was assumed that they couldn't. Along with their research work, they formed the International Association for the Scientific Study of Mental Deficiency (IASSMD), as it was called then. It is now called the International Association for the Scientific Study of Intellectual Disability (IASSID). The Congress meets every four years in different parts of the world and the first public presentation of my work was at the Congress in Dublin in 1988. That presentation was about individual therapy outcomes and is reported in my 1989 publication *Meeting the needs of handicapped people: a psychodynamic approach.* It was the first report of the application of the stage model. It was about individual therapy at that time.

The work that proved the learning capacity of people with limited cognitive ability led to the development of day centres for adults with intellectual disabilities.

Following on from work with adults with intellectual disabilities, there was a growing recognition of the needs of children, many of whom were institutionalised. It was not uncommon for paediatricians to say to mothers of disabled children that they should leave them at the hospital and go home and make another one. There were many children who only ever had an institutionalised life. Some of those will be the ones that I knew in my childhood, who were stuck at a very early stage of emotional development, almost certainly caused by their lack of individual emotional care in babyhood and early childhood. The research continued through the 1950s and 60s, and led to the Education Act of 1970, which was the forerunner to the special schools and the provision of education for all children, regardless of the level of their cognitive impairment. This has made a huge difference to the lives of people with disabilities and their families.

These developments are all seen as positive. However, from the perspective of this book, there was still a propensity to be very behavioural. BF Skinner, with his applied behaviour analysis, was very active at the same time and there was certainly an attraction in having a way forward that was demonstrated to be effective. And there is no doubt that applied behaviour analysis, used properly with the right people at the right time, can be very effective. My argument is always that it needs to be applied within the context of supportive positive relationships, and that there is no point using a behavioural approach with anyone who is emotionally pre-rapprochement, as they may be unable to respond to praise. Developmentally, children need to have reached a stage at which they value the opinions of somebody else, and can relate at a two-person level, before they can respond to behavioural approaches. That doesn't mean that they wouldn't respond to being treated negatively, but the idea of behavioural approaches in terms of teaching appropriate behaviour is that they should respond to it positivity. And, of course, anything perceived negatively can be further traumatising. The behavioural movement was huge and is still used today in lots of fields where we are aiming to increase a specific behaviour. Some very modern examples are online gambling and video game addiction.

During my masters degree, I was engaged in delivering the Bereweeke scheme to a small group home for children with profound disabilities. This was a very detailed behavioural scheme that identified a particular skill that might be possible to achieve in 13 weeks. The stages of the skill development were broken down into 13 parts, relevant paperwork put together and the programme followed to see what could be achieved. This was quite a satisfying piece of work and the little children showed remarkable responses. One, with cerebral palsy and no verbal language, completed all 13 parts in the first week, which showed us that he did not in fact have a cognitive impairment. This was very exciting and led to him moving into a special school for children with physical disabilities. The other notable and equally exciting event was a profoundly disabled boy who was able to show, when given the opportunity, that he did have some conscious control of one hand from the elbow, and could raise his hand to pull things towards him. Once we knew that he had this conscious control, we could, of course, use that as a communication for 'yes' and 'no'. Having the ability to indicate yes and no is remarkably freeing for someone with profound physical disabilities. He began to respond well to opportunities for choice about food, activity, what to wear, whether it was too hot or too cold, and so on. Without this scheme we would never have discovered these issues.

I am not aware of anyone using the Bereweeke scheme now, but I think that positive behaviour support programmes can address similar issues in a similar way. The important thing is to be systematic, evaluating all the time, being very alert to subtle changes in behaviour that indicate a response. I have had the misfortune, at times, to be in facilities for a number of people with profound physical and intellectual disabilities. I find them to be very depressing places with a sense of hopelessness, because it is so difficult to know how to help. Services tend to focus primarily on physical care with little knowledge about how to address cognitive or emotional needs. It is possible, through observation, to assess a person's emotional developmental stage, provide care that matches that stage, with the possibility of progressing to a more advanced stage. There are, of course, ways of providing physical care that can be nurturing and positive, but sadly it is often the case that, if two carers are needed, they speak to each other rather than the person they are helping. Some of this will be because of the emotional strain of the work that they are doing, and it is important that all service providers take good care of their support staff if they want them to provide an emotionally nurturing environment for the people they are supporting.

The middle of the 20th century was a period of rapid and extensive development in services and approaches, much of it positive. Findings on learning capacity, and the development of education and adult day centres, led to investigations into more appropriate ways to provide services. At the same time there were some scandals involving ill-treatment in the old long-stay hospitals, and this led to the Community Care Act of 1979 and the closure programme in which I was much involved. I helped to close ten hospitals in my NHS career. There is an excellent book called *Hospitals in Trouble*, by JP Martin, which charts the decline of several large hospitals at which people with intellectual disabilities were ill-treated and exploited with physical, sexual and financial abuse. All of these cases will, of course, have included emotional abuse, as the helplessness of the people concerned would leave them very vulnerable. It was a time of shame.

There was an investment in research which was very helpful. Emerson, Felce and Mansell became well-known leaders of the research into community care. They showed that, as long as there is sufficient investment, financially and expertly, then the majority of people with intellectual disabilities can live in ordinary houses with ordinary support. Mansell was commissioned to gather evidence and provide a report on what became known as 'challenging behaviour'. This term has survived for many years and is still used in education, healthcare and social care settings to refer to people whose behaviour is a challenge to others. Sadly, it has become almost a diagnosis rather than a recognition that it is the other people who are challenged, not the individual. It is my contention that the people whose behaviour is difficult to understand or tolerate are the ones who are emotionally disabled, suffering anxiety from trauma that they can neither understand nor process.

There was a shift from healthcare to social care at this time and the term 'normalisation' became widely used. The idea was that people with intellectual disabilities should have the same normal opportunities as others, and be treated as normally as possible. This was largely a good thing, but sadly did not reach the people who were not able to respond to the opportunities that were offered. And I contest that these individuals are the ones who are emotionally disabled, who can't, because of their early trauma, recognise and appreciate the opportunities that were made available to them. Positive programming is something that was developed for specialist support programmes for more complex needs and it did address some of them. Intensive support teams were set up in the community and some of them were very effective. As always, they were subject to financial pressures and many were absorbed into community teams, sometimes losing their focus. It is now variable in most areas, as to whether there is an intensive support team in all areas of the country. The positive programming developed by Donnellan and Lavinia was the forerunner to the present positive behaviour support that is now recognised by NICE as the approach of choice for people with intellectual disabilities. It has become the focus of attention of most services. And most of it is very positive, although, again, it struggles to take account of the emotional needs of people who are traumatised before the individuation stage of development.

If asked to use a PBS approach with an individual, I have found it possible to use the model to describe ways of working that can be beneficial for the individual. So, it would follow that a possible aim within the PBS plan would be "to provide an emotionally nurturing environment" and then go on to describe how this is done by providing a significant other person to be available at all times, and to then describe ways of working that match with the emotional developmental stage that the person had reached. This is slightly different from the way I have seen some PBS programmes written. It has been my experience over many years, that long-worded documents tend not to be put into practice, and I get disturbed by some of the plans that I see prepared, as there is very little likelihood that direct support staff will have time to read it never mind put it into action. The sort of approach that follows from the trauma informed care model, on the other hand, can be put forward in very simple language and can be followed by relatively untrained support staff who have a basic compassion for the people they are supporting.

Professor Clark and his colleagues made a huge difference to the way that services were seen in the mid-20th century. However, there can be no doubt that the constant reworking and relabelling is a response to the stress of trauma. It is the most distressed and traumatised people who end up in the most restrictive environments, often within segregated facilities with locked doors and other restrictions. It is possible, within such environments, to provide an emotionally nurturing experience. It depends on the way that it is done. If you have someone who is emotionally less than one year old, but in a 25-year-old's body, big and strong, then it may be necessary to provide a very restricted environment, physically, but it is still possible to provide emotional support equivalent to what would be provided to a toddler in a pram. It is important to maintain the adult language, and to facilitate cognitive development, or make sure it's not lost. But at the same time, keeping the world safe, with compassion, is the vital work that is required. If an individual is so traumatised from their early life that they make little progress, they can still be provided with a very safe environment in a community setting. This would need to have the oversight of the court of protection to ensure that it is right and not cruel. The secret is to provide emotional security. It requires physical security as well. It is the way that it is provided that matters. I have seen services that are close to a prison-type regime, where the person is being told all the time what to do and what not to do. Sometimes people are physically restrained or forced into activities like showering and moving from room to room. I have also seen services in which the individual has not wanted to leave the safety of the provision, even when encouraged to go out and about. It is, of course, important to provide opportunities for people to explore the world, and certainly those early pioneers were looking to ways to enable people to have bigger lives and be visible in the community. Much has been achieved, but there is further to go, and the big issue is the recognition of the importance of a person's emotional developmental needs.

Chapter 3: Understanding an individual's emotional disability

Here, we take the story further to explore more recent material and the thinking behind the model of emotional disability.

Over the years of using the model with people with intellectual disabilities, and working in a wider field of emotional distress, it has become clear to me that issues of emotional development are key to all of us. If a person has what they need in the first few years of life, they can reach a stage of psychological birth, a sense of themself as a whole person, and this takes them through their whole life.

I started to use the term 'emotional disability' a few years ago, particularly in relation to people with a diagnosis of emotionally unstable personality disorder (EU PD). It became clear to me that these individuals did not have a secure sense of themselves as a whole person. Their frequent mood changes, sometimes from one extreme to another, was very much like what we see in toddlers, when one minute they can be happy and smiling, and the next minute screaming and distressed. In toddlers, we understand this to be a response to something they either don't understand or can't tolerate. And in those with an intellectual disability, we tend to think that they can't be expected to understand. But in people without an intellectual disability, we are left wondering what has happened to leave them unable to tolerate much of ordinary life.

We need to take the model of healthy emotional development and recognise it at a much broader level. This can then inform primary childcare practices, parenting support and all aspects of society, giving everyone the best chance, and the best start, in life. We know from the writings of Winnicott, Bowlby, Klien, Mahler and others, that we can observe the impact of early life experiences on child development. It has always been a concern to me that most of the milestones recorded during the early years are based on physical and cognitive development. There is some recognition of the development of sociability, social interaction and communication. However, in my experience of working with early years workers, most of them have not been introduced to the subtleties of the primary interaction and development of self.

In an ideal world, all babies and toddlers would receive what they need from people who know how to provide it. But parenthood is one of the jobs in life that we can all choose to do, or most of us can, without any qualifications. For most of us, our first child, and the intense needs of a newborn baby, come as a shock. I can speak from my own experience here! That tiny bundle of humanity that cries without being able to tell you what they're crying about puts massive demands on the new parent. So, we can reflect on what it must be like for the tiny baby, helpless to get its needs met, and completely dependent on the adults around them. I suspect it is too painful for most of us to reflect too deeply on what it was like to be so helpless. Although many of us will go back to that stage with advanced years and/or advanced dementia. More on that later...

It is important for us all to realise that trauma is idiosyncratic. Any of us can be traumatised by something unexpected or not understood. If we think about it in that way, it becomes easier to accept that small babies and toddlers can be traumatised by relatively small events. It doesn't need to be a major accident or serious incident. It can be an event that seems quite normal to the adults around them. As mentioned, one of the things that is commonly experienced as traumatic is the arrival of a sibling. Most of us who have more than one child are aware of the shock that the first child, who has been the centre of the universe for maybe a couple of years, experiences when a new baby comes into the house. The toddler does not understand why the baby makes so much noise or needs so much attention. And they will have an idiosyncratic response to this change in their lives. If they have an intellectual disability, their response may be not understood in quite the same way. But with or without an intellectual disability, they will be affected. And there are, of course, many other events that can be experienced as traumatic. For example, mum needing to go to hospital or to leave the house for other reasons, mum and dad falling out, more people in the household creating confusion, not enough to eat or keep warm. All of these things can be relatively normal and ordinary, but are experienced, or can be experienced, as traumatic by the little child that doesn't understand what is going on.

I find it helpful when assessing the impact of early trauma, to use a number of assessment tools. The FAIT is the obvious one, as that has been developed specifically for this purpose. But I also find it useful to use the House Tree Person test (HTP) or the Object Relations Technique (ORT).

The ORT is perhaps more applicable to an adult population without intellectual disabilities. There are 13 cards in the test, and the subject is asked to say what picture they can see on each card, what they think is happening, and what they think will happen next. The cards have pictures that include one person, two people, three people or a group. The stories that have been generated are then analysed to see if there is a stage where the person has got stuck, which indicates trauma. A brief summary suggests that disturbance at the one-person level indicates very primary trauma and may be associated with psychopathy, serious psychotic conditions, or intense autism. Disturbance at the two-person level is associated with bipolar disorders and EU PD. Disturbance at the three-person level is associated with depression and anxiety, with disturbance of the group level suggesting early development has been good enough, with some dramatic life experiences at a later stage. We would always hope that people have a sense of who they are and where they fit in the world by the time they get to school, which is the time at which they need to function at the group level. Although the ORT is perhaps a more appropriate tool to use with non-intellectually disabled people; an observation of behaviour using the FAIT would show the same issues and allow for a diagnosis of a stuck stage.

We will look at the other test, the HTP, later.

There have been many models of understanding mental health difficulties over the years, and different approaches to trying to help and support people who have emotional distress. We have gone from rejecting models to institutional models to community care, to a wider awareness of the need to look after our mental health. There does not seem, however, to be enough attention paid to enabling people to develop good mental health in childhood. There has been quite a lot of attention paid to recommending appropriate diets for children for healthy growth and development, concentrating on physical needs, although these have slipped in recent times with the overuse of processed food and the consequent development of obesity. There have been attempts at times to be more understanding of mental health issues, and certainly of the impact of trauma on people who serve in the armed forces, experience road traffic accidents, or other violent experiences that can be seen by most people to be traumatic.

What seems to be the case, and is not easily recognised in my experience, is that people who have had a good early experience, and passed through the emotional developmental stages successfully, are more resilient to dealing with trauma in later life. It follows, logically, that if we attend to the healthy development of self, the establishment of a strong emotional self in the early years, before starting school, children and young people would have a better chance of being resilient in the future.

I find it helpful to recognise the toddler inside the adult person I am interacting with. This doesn't mean that I draw that to their attention as that would be distressing. What it does mean is that I accept that something traumatic has happened in their early life, that they have managed to mask, often for many years, and that this has led to them needing to hide from something that they probably don't understand. When people come for therapy, they often have a relatively superficial grasp on why they feel the way they do, but usually respond very quickly with a deeper understanding once made aware of the impact of early life events on our ability to function as adults.

There is even more relevance for the model of emotional development in what we see in dementia, except here the stages are followed in reverse order as the brain ceases to function. This seems to hold for all the different dementias, although there are specific differences that may require additional interventions. But if the individual with dementia can receive the emotional support that matches their emotional developmental stage, their lives will be enhanced.

At the top of the model of emotional development is individuation, that state of knowing oneself and where one fits in world, that is hopefully achieved by the time a child goes to school and usually by the age of four. If achieved, that stable emotional state is maintained throughout life, but with the onset of dementia comes the need for additional support. The late rapprochement stage, which comes just before individuation, is the stage of accepting and using interaction with another person to achieve goals. The person with dementia who is just beginning to lose their independence will go into this stage of asking for help, accepting that they need help, and have an awareness of what is happening to them. As they deteriorate further, they move into the early rapprochement stage at which they become quite demanding, expecting others to meet their needs, usually immediately! As they deteriorate further, they move into a more insular state of repetitive behaviours with little reference to the importance of another person. At this stage, they still need to know that someone else is there, keeping the world safe, and this is perhaps the most demanding stage for families and staff to manage. There is the sadness of the person disappearing, and the inability to make it right, together with the irritation of the repetitive nature of the behaviour. Further deterioration leads to the differentiation stage, where the person is completely self-referenced, often bedbound, and needing to be cared for like a young baby. Their physical needs then become the focus of care and support as, to a large extent, the individual's personality has gone. The pattern becomes similar to that of a newborn, with food, change, sleep, and repeat. If the emotional support for each stage is provided adequately, there can be a huge reduction in anxiety and distress for both the individual and the carers. I find it distressing, personally, when I find staff or families trying to reason with somebody who has already deteriorated to the early rapprochement or even earlier stages. It causes distress on all sides.

I wonder if services could be reframed and more appropriately provided if we could accept a model of emotional disability instead of mental illness, and if we could recognise that child development, emotional security and care in early childhood is crucial to the development of emotionally healthy adults.

The work and research that has gone into the development of the FAIT has been with people with intellectual disabilities and is still crucial in that field. Most of the following chapters refer to people with intellectual disabilities as they are the people I have most knowledge of and had longer-term involvement with. It just seemed really important to add this chapter about the wider application, which may benefit the whole of society if it were recognised. There are some stories later to expand on this theme.

Chapter 4: What the Frankish Assessment of the Impact of Trauma (FAIT) is and how to use it

Looking at the development and content of the Frankish Assessment of the Impact of Trauma.

This work is very much based on the model of psychological birth that Margaret Mahler put forward. She worked as a psychoanalyst in the United States in the 1970s, setting up a laboratory to observe children from birth to five years old with their primary carers. Through these observations, Mahler was able to understand the stages of emotional development that a child goes through. She was also able to describe the behaviours seen at each stage. This latter point is crucial for an understanding of delayed emotional development.

Mahler and her colleagues wrote up this work in a book called *The Psychological Birth of the Human Infant* (1979). This book describes the stages from biological birth, when the baby is born, through to the child's psychological birth. This is the point when the child has an individual identity of its own. This usually happens around three-and-a-half years old. Mahler *et al* called the psychological birth the point of individuation. This is very similar to what Winnicott described as 'rationalisation'. This is when the child has gone through the emotional developmental stages and can think clearly about itself within its environment.

I have adapted Mahler's work to thinking about people with intellectual disabilities and I describe how people can become stuck at a different stages of emotional development. We are going to look now at the Mahler stages in neurotypical development. Most of the rest of this book is about the use of the model and its impact on people.

Mahler's stages

The first is the symbiotic stage and is the newborn period in the first few weeks of life. At this stage, it is as if the mother and child are still connected. This is the stage that Winnicott described when the mother and child are in a very close enmeshed relationship. In the symbiotic stage, the child is entirely dependent on its mother to have its needs met.

The next stage is called differentiation, when the baby develops an awareness of itself and the parts of its body. This stage starts at a few weeks and goes on to about nine months. At this stage, babies will look at and play with their hands, feet or sometimes their genitals. They also become aware of their immediate surroundings such as the cot or pram that they are in and the toys that are around them. At this stage, the baby is only aware of a very small space around it and begins to notice that it exists within this small space.

The behaviours seen in the differentiation stage are called self-referenced behaviours. This means that everything the baby does is in reference to itself. It doesn't do anything to influence anybody else except in the sense that it cries and screams, and it does so because it wants something for itself, for example it is hungry, wet or cold. The baby therefore is only aware of other people being around in terms of getting its own needs met.

Brain development in babies happens very quickly. Through this rapid brain development, the baby becomes able to do new things on a very regular basis. Mahler and her colleagues found that the baby will start to practice a new skill as it becomes available. The baby will practice the new skill again and again until it can do it well. Examples of this include throwing its toy out of the pram and doing so again and again. Other behaviours will be rolling over, crawling and standing up.

This stage begins at around nine months and continues to around 15 months. The baby may practice behaviours at other times, but this is the main practising stage. When the child can engage in a particular behaviour well, another becomes available due to the rapid brain development. The child then begins practising this new behaviour, and the previous behaviour slots into their repertoire of available behaviours.

It is very important in the practising stage that someone is around watching and paying attention to the child. Mahler found that if the child knew it was being watched, then the practising behaviour continued. If the child thought that nobody was paying attention, they practised much less. This would make learning a new behaviour much slower.

The next stage is the rapprochement stage. The word 'rapprochement' means give and take. Give and take is one of the most important skills needed in relationships. In this stage, the child is beginning to have a two-way, or reciprocal, relationship with its primary carers. This stage is divided into two sub-stages, early rapprochement and late rapprochement. It goes from about 15 months to about three-and-a-half years.

The early rapprochement stage is the start of the child beginning to learn the concept of give and take. This begins around 15 months and goes on until about two years. The first sign that a child has moved into the early rapprochement stage is when the child begins to say no or walks away. This shows the start of two-way negotiation. The child moving into this stage can be challenging for the parents and it is sometimes called the 'terrible twos'.

In this stage the child will become interested in peekaboo and round and round the garden games. These games are about two-way communication and give and take between two people.

The late rapprochement stage is the beginning of the child moving towards independence. This stage can be more challenging as the child is negotiating and can be demanding about getting its needs met. This happens from two to three years.

In this stage, the child also gradually begins to increase the distance it can be away from the primary carers or parents. It can do this with its levels of anxiety being manageable. This is similar to the ideas of Winnicott and Bowlby, who talked about the child gradually having the confidence to move away from the mother or safe base, and explore the world.

It is important that the child's anxiety is manageable, so they are not overwhelmed. Independence grows in small steps that the child can cope with. For example, at playgroup, the child may start off being sat by its mother's feet. When it is a few months older, the child will move away to play with the other children in the middle of the floor. It can do this by being able to keep an eye on mum and where she is. As the child moves into later rapprochement, it will be able to go a bit further away from her still. It can do this without being anxious about where she is.

Emotional refuelling is important in this stage to help the child feel confident. This is where the child will look round for the parent and make eye contact. This eye contact will emotionally refuel the child and help them feel confident. They can then happily carry on playing at a distance from the carer.

In having the confidence to move away from the carer the child can begin to explore. Through this the child is learning about the world around it. The child is also beginning to understand its own place in the world.

Once the child has moved fairly smoothly through the stages above, it reaches the individuation stage. This is the point where the child can be separate from the primary carer with manageable anxiety. Note that this is not a state of having no anxiety. It is normal, and indeed sometimes helpful, to have some manageable anxiety. It is more a state of not being overwhelmed by anxiety when separated from the parent or primary carer.

Some children reach the individuation stage through a rapprochement crisis. This is when they realise the primary carer is not there, they become anxious, distressed and may have a tantrum. They then realise that they can cope with the situation. Individuation is the point of the child knowing that they are separate from the carer but that they can manage their anxiety.

Reaching the individuation stage is the psychological birth of the child. That is the point at which they have reached their own identity, as being separate from their parents. At this point, the child is psychologically able to grow further into an independent human being, who can stand on their own two feet.

Margaret Mahler helps us to understand the stages that a child goes through to reach individuation. She helps us to know what behaviours can be seen at each stage. It is therefore possible, by observing the behaviour of a child, to work out what stage of emotional development they are at.

These stages will be referred to in the following chapters, which include stories of people who have benefited from an understanding of the emotional development model.

How to use the FAIT

The development of the FAIT took many years and became the work of my doctoral study. Having found the model in Mahler's descriptions of the developmental stages. Initially, I set about observing children in their natural environments to see if I could ascertain the developmental stage at which they might be stuck. Initially, I observed a little boy for six hours in three different environments of two hours each. What he actually did in the different environments was very different, but it became clear that the way that he did what he did was constant across the different environments and represented the emotional developmental stage at which he was stuck. These observations were clearly very time-consuming and, as the stage was the same in the different environments, it raised the question of the need to establish the specific behaviours, as opposed to the type of behaviour. The type of behaviour was what mattered.

I then went on to recruit assistant psychologists to do more observations of different people in different environments, including different ages. A great deal of data was collected and was analysed using the Kappa Statistical analysis method. What that showed, which was a surprise – and a pleasant surprise – was that the result was established after 40 minutes of observation and didn't change no matter how much longer the observation continued. This meant that a 40-minute observation could reliably provide the information about the stage of emotional development at which a child was stuck. It was also established that time sampling of observing for 20 seconds, and writing for 40 seconds, continuing for 40 minutes, would give a reliable result. Clearly, what I'm covering in this one short paragraph was many hours of work, which proved to be very rewarding in the end.

Interrater reliability was also tested with the same group of observers. Two people would observe the same person, and what they saw wasn't necessarily the same thing, but, again, the category of behaviours was the same, thus providing further confirmation of the reliability of the measure. The next big question was validity, and a reference group was established including a range of professionals in the field relevant to the study and, after several meetings, they were happy that what was being done in the assessment was valid.

The process is therefore that an individual is observed for 40 minutes in their natural environment, although the environment does not seem to be terribly relevant. There is the question of consent to be observed, and people can be asked or relevant people be asked to respond on the grounds of best practice. There is no risk of any harm being done to the person being observed. It can be interesting if the person being observed wants to interact with the observer. Clearly, if this happens, then it is recorded as a relevant behaviour, and would be, of course, a rapprochement behaviour.

Once the 40 observations have been recorded, they are then scored. The measurement tool does not use symbiosis or individuation, only the four points of differentiation, practising, early rapprochement and late rapprochement. It is very rare to see someone at the symbiotic stage, and people who are individuated are unlikely to be referred. Once the observations have been allocated a number for a stage, scores are added up and the highest number indicates the stage at which the person is functioning. It is quite common to find that the highest scores are in practising and early rapprochement, indicating that this is a common stage at which to get stuck.

When there is a clear indication that the person may be moving between two stages, for example if they score 18 on practising and 16 on early rapprochement with the occasional differentiation and late rapprochement behaviour, then clearly they are moving into the rapprochement stage. The implication for an intervention is that they need lots of practising opportunities within the context of early rapprochement, opportunities for discussion, sharing and negotiation. Someone with a clear high score in practising would need an intervention based on lots of practising behaviours and opportunities, with staff or parents being alert to signs of rapprochement developing. One of the critical points is that, if there is an expectation of rapprochement ability before it is there, the individual will react negatively because they will not feel sufficiently looked after. This group probably represents the largest group of referrals.

I have stressed the need to recognise that it is the category of behaviours that matters, rather than the specific behaviour itself. This is crucial as we often observe the same behaviour with a different meaning. One of the examples that I give when teaching is that of headbanging. Headbanging at the differentiation stage is self-referenced and is not conveying anything to another person. Headbanging at the practising stage, is a behaviour that the person knows how to do and hasn't developed another behaviour to take its place. Headbanging at the early rapprochement stage is a cry for help. Headbanging at the late rapprochement stage is saying, "you'd better do something" and is indicative of the fact that the person recognises that someone else can intervene in their life.

It is important to note again the need to recognise the meaning of behaviour and to respond accordingly. A behavioural approach would often say to ignore behaviours that are inappropriate, and reward those that are appropriate. What this model says is that all behaviour has meaning and none of it should be ignored. Anyone with delayed emotional development at pre-individuation will respond painfully to being ignored.

It was a huge surprise to find that 40 minutes of observation could give such rich information on which interventions could be based. Some people still find it hard to accept that it is valid and reliable. However, in my own experience, and the experience of many colleagues, we have found that it does work. Clearly, one of the significant factors that works is providing the availability of a significant other for anyone who is pre-individuation in their emotional development. It seems that this has been counterintuitive in the past, with the emphasis being on behavioural approaches, as providing more attention has been seen as the wrong thing to do. It has long been my position that people who are described as 'attention seeking' are in fact 'attention needing', and if the need for confirmation of self is provided by the availability of a reliable significant other, there can be rapid progress.

There is a projective test, mentioned briefly earlier, called the House Tree Person (HTP), which is often added to the assessment. This must be used very carefully as the individual gives away a lot about themselves in their drawings. To administer it, you need to offer one sheet of paper and ask them to draw a house, take that away out of sight, provide a second sheet of paper and ask them to draw a tree. Again, remove the paper and then give them a third and ask them to draw a person. The house is indicative of basic security and most people draw a house with four windows and door and roof and chimney. Deviations from that have meaning. The tree needs to have roots, a strong trunk and a significant top. Again, no roots indicates denial of the past, a strong trunk denotes a good healthy ego, and a substantial top indicates positive ego development. The person is indicative of the identity and needs to have a body, arms legs, hands and feet, features on the face and look like a person. Over the years, I have seen many variations on the themes and found this test to be very reliable in recording the difficulties, and then, with a retest, progress in therapy. The original HTP was developed for use in therapy with children but I have developed it as an assessment tool for people with intellectual disabilities.

It must be remembered that people are stuck because of something traumatic that has happened in their life. This means that, as well as being stuck in their emotional development, there are other factors that may need exploration for recovery to happen. At times, there is a need for individual therapy as well. It is worth remembering that all of this work came about because of the shortage of availability of individual therapy for people with trauma in their lives. The first group of people I worked with, with this model, were individuals receiving individual therapy, and I reported this work in my paper of 1989. This led to the development of an approach that can be provided more widely, and by staff trained in the model, which are much more available than psychotherapists. Experience has shown that *training* of a staff group in a school or a care facility fundamentally shifts the approach they have to their charges with emotional developmental delay. The really positive outcome is the reduction in distressed behaviour and the progress to more mature emotional development. It remains difficult to enable people to reach full individuation, but if they reach late rapprochement, the quality of their life is significantly improved by their ability to negotiate and to respond to requests to share.

The FAIT is available with a manual, and training can be purchased. A community of practice has also been established to facilitate discussion and application to a wider group of people. It has long been my hope that emotional developmental delay as a result of trauma will be recognised in the design of support packages for people with complex behaviour. Most of these will have a level of intellectual disability as well, but not all. There is relevance for most people who present with psychological difficulties. Throughout the rest of this book will be stories of people who have benefited from the use of the FAIT and the recognition of their emotional needs.

Case studies

Chapter 5: Joanne

Here we meet our first example of the application of the model of emotional disability – a young person with severely self-harming behaviour.

This nine-year-old girl was referred by her school because of severe self-injurious behaviour. She attended a special school for children with special needs, and a major problem involved transportation to and from school. When distressed, she would batter her head with her fists, her knees, inanimate objects and anything she could find, leaving her head, ears and face covered in bruises and abrasions. It was very distressing to see her in that condition, and even more distressing to see the level of emotional pain she was experiencing when inflicting physical pain on herself. At one stage she had cauliflower ears like a boxer.

Joanne reminded me of a young girl I had known when working as a temporary nursing assistant during university vacations. This young girl was a patient on a ward of 15 children under 16, and didn't walk so shuffled around on the floor. Every now and again we would realise that she wasn't present in the day room, and on looking for her, would find that she had shuffled onto the veranda and was bashing her head on the floor in a state of extreme distress. At the time, before much of my own training, I did not understand or have a model for understanding what was going on for her. I did understand on a human level that she was extremely unhappy and had no other means of expressing her despair. She was quite small so I would pick her up and sit rocking her until she calmed and would then take a drink and be more settled for a while. But she stayed with me in my consciousness as someone that I didn't understand and wasn't able to give significant help to at time.

Meeting Joanne many years later, after much study and research, I felt in a much stronger position to be able to help. I began by visiting her at school and at home with her family. I carried out my observations of her behaviour so as to establish the level of emotional development according to Mahler's theory captured by the FAIT. The observation showed that her behaviours predominantly fell into the differentiation stage of emotional development. This is, of course, a very early stage, belonging to the first few months of life. This led to the question of what could have happened to her at the beginning of her life to result in her being stuck in her emotional development. It should be noted here that, intellectually, she was more able – able to talk, write and draw, read a little, and use electronic devices quite competently. One of her comforts was engaging with characters on her electronic device.

I spoke with the teachers and they were definitely struggling to know how to help, as well as facing their own distress seeing the child so distressed. They were questioning their own ability to provide an education for her. It was so difficult to help her to concentrate and work on learning without provoking, accidentally, a further episode of self-harm.

I then spoke with her parents, primarily her mother, although her father and sister were clearly supportive, too. Her sister was younger but, having had the experience of living with her sister for all her life, she was able to tolerate what she saw without becoming too distressed herself. Grandparents lived nearby and supported significantly. This was especially helpful for the younger sister to go to her grandma when her big sister was having a bad day.

I asked an open question of mum: "Can you think of anything that distressed Joanne before the age of five?" Although I knew I was looking at a much earlier stage than five, I wanted the question to be as open as possible, and not to be a leading question. Mum immediately responded with, "I couldn't feed her". She then went on to say that Joanne's first few weeks of life had been very stressful, that she wouldn't feed, or couldn't feed, and mum, with her first baby, didn't know what to do. She had clearly been traumatised herself by this experience as well as her daughter. We explored this in more detail, and it became clear to me that the experience of the difficulty with feeding had seriously interfered with Joanne's development of attachment, trust and early emotional development. This is a very painful subject to discuss with parents who have done their best for their child and who may not have had the right or useful advice from professionals at the time. This young mum had not felt able to ask for help and had struggled on as best she could. She understood that her daughter had a diagnosis of autism and was connecting this with the self-harming behaviour. And there clearly is a link, but not all autistic children self-harm, so it isn't part of the condition, and the reason must lie elsewhere. I was able to explain the findings from my observations and gently talk through the options for helping Joanne to recover. It was important, as it always is, that the family and the school staff were supportive of the proposed intervention.

From my experience of disability psychotherapy over many years, I had confidence in an approach that could work. This would include making sure that her day-to-day experiences were supportive of her development of self, and that individual psychotherapy was available to her to provide an opportunity for her to 'grow again' from that early position, equivalent to a relatively newborn baby. This approach was new for the school staff but they took on the role with enthusiasm. It is worth noting here that the school staff all took on training in the model and adopted it with enthusiasm, using it with lots of the children, with good results.

One part of the early exploratory work was to examine the issue of transport. I travelled with Joanne on her journey to school so that I could become aware of what was causing her distress. It became clear very quickly that she struggled to cope with anything unexpected and would react with panic. I started a commentary on what was happening, keeping up a dialogue all the time, describing what was happening outside of the vehicle, and predicting where possible what would happen next. I asked the driver to always put the indicator on in good time before changing direction so that Joanne would begin to link the sound of the indicator with the change of direction and not be alarmed when it happened. Putting this sort of certainty into her life made a difference, so training the driver and the escort to follow this pattern stopped self-harm on journeys. For Joanne, it was an issue of feeling safe and could be linked back to the feelings of extreme fear she had experienced as a baby that she would not be able to express at the pre-verbal level. The implication is that she had some pre-verbal memories of being in vehicles when she was in pain.

The next thing to establish was individual psychotherapy and this was undertaken first of all in school. Joanne would spend time with me in a small room adjoining her classroom. Sometimes she would draw, sometimes talk and draw, and mostly her drawings were of characters from her digital world. There seemed to be a need for her to spend much of her time in an alternative world from the day-to-day experience of living. She responded well to the individual time and attention, always happy to see me and always attentive. She would talk through most of the session, controlling the space, which was clearly important to her. I was able, of course, to let this happen within the understanding of the nature of the therapy, which was to give her, as much as possible, the experience of being the omnipotent baby who has their needs met unconditionally. Sessions were never more than half an hour, and she would tell me when it was time to go. When I left, she would always say that I would see her again next time, giving herself the reassurance that it was okay to send me away, and that I would still return with the same positive regard for her.

During this time, a decision was made for Joanne to move to another school, one that specialised in autism. The big question that arose was about transport as the new school was a further distance away. We were optimistic that the narrative approach would work and, in fact, it did. There could still be difficulties if there were major delays on the journey, but generally speaking all went well. Joanne was able to become a weekly boarder, travelling to school on Monday mornings and back on Friday afternoons. This meant that her therapy sessions moved to Friday late afternoons after her return from school. I saw her at home, usually in her parents' bedroom, which was where the computer lived, and she could continue to interact with the computer while talking to me. She did have her own computer downstairs but the space was less private. Over time, she did move on to being seen in her own room without a computer. And after a further few months, she became able to share the bedroom with her sister. This was a significant move forward emotionally into a more mature developmental stage.

During this time, school reviews indicated that Joanne was making progress in her learning and in her tolerance of other children. She continued to be quite egocentric, as would be expected from her emotional developmental level, but her ability to see and respond to other children gradually improved. As a severely autistic child sharing her educational space with other autistic children, there was never likely to be a huge amount of social interaction. However, there was some, and that was progress.

I continued to attend reviews at school to keep up to date with what was happening there, and to feed in what I was finding in my individual sessions. Working together clearly benefited everyone, and the time commitment could be justified, as, once therapy started, there was no more severe self-injury. Joanne would occasionally hit herself but never to the extent that she had been doing when I first knew her. School staff did not necessarily fully comprehend the psychodynamic model.

However, they were pleased to see the progress that Joanne was making. She remained very attached to electronic devices and would put pressure on teaching staff to take her to the IT room. This became better regulated over time, and school staff were able to see the significance of nonhuman interaction for Joanne. It was a crucial part of her recovery, but people could understand her struggle to read, interact with, and understand other people. Her need to be omnipotent, in charge, was always there, and still is to some extent, but her tolerance of other people has increased over time.

Progress in school continued, and, over time, it became clear that Joanne was more intellectually and cognitively able than had first been surmised. She has, therefore, gone on to study for exams at entry level with some success.

Individual sessions at home continued for a while, until one day there was a significant session during which she had what can only be described as an existential crisis, and hence the huge turning point for her. We were sitting in her parents' bedroom with her looking at the computer screen and me sitting beside her, although she had graduated to let me sit beside the table so that I could look at her and we could make eye contact. (This was itself a significant improvement from when we first started therapy.) This particular day the computer was not going as she wished, and she was becoming frustrated. I could see the tension building up in her and knew that, in the past, this would have led to a major battering of her head. But on this occasion, I could see her arguing with herself in her head, and gradually taking control so as not to explode. I was able to say, quietly, "Well done", and she made eye contact and relaxed. She was clearly aware of what she had done and I was clearly aware but it didn't need talking about.

And that was the beginning of the end of our therapy relationship. I did see her for a couple more sessions but there was clearly no work to do. She had progressed, emotionally, to a level that we call early rapprochement, where she could interact with another person and see the point of that interaction as being two-way and not just her having her needs that.

The process of moving from differentiation to early rapprochement in neurotypical development takes about 18 months. This intervention took approximately the same time, and this seems to be one of the findings from using the approach. But the critical factor is that there is no evidence that it would have happened, that progress would be made, had the direct intervention not taken place.

We can reflect on what might have happened with the child who was so severely self-injuring had we not been able to put in place a targeted intervention based on an understanding of early trauma. It is very hard for any of us to think that a young baby has been traumatised. But there is increasing evidence from clinical work that the people who are traumatised at the pre-verbal level do seem to be the ones who go on to seriously harm themselves, property, or other people. As this group are the most expensive to support, the most distressing to be with, and cause tremendous distress to their families, we owe it to them to pursue a model of intervention that has been shown to work.

It has been extremely difficult for services to accept that trauma can happen at a very early age, perhaps because it is too painful to think about a fragile little baby suffering trauma. And we know that psychoanalysis is not readily available, and that the language used is often not easily accepted. It became important to me, and was very much led by my reading of Mahler's work, to find a way of bringing the theory to practice in a way that is readily acceptable to frontline staff in education and care. The FAIT is the result of that work.

Chapter 6: Freddie

An introduction to the early work on the model of understanding.

Freddie was a little boy who became an essential part of the development of the FAIT. He was first referred to me when he was about six years old and attending a special school where I provided some psychology services. I was at the school one day when he arrived with his mum, strapped into a buggy. He was then pushed through the door, two staff grabbed an arm each, carried him through to the changing room, changed him into play clothes, and then put him out in the garden. On enquiry, I was told that this was the only way to stop him wrecking the whole school. I watched him out in the garden as he dug soil and poured it over himself. He was clearly a distressed little boy and unable to relate to people.

I decided to observe him in different settings with different people. This was at school, at home, and at the respite care service that he attended two days a week and alternate weekends. One of the things that became clear from the observations was that he could not tolerate things being on top of other things, and any surface had to be cleared instantly with everything ending up on the floor. Clearly, this was a behaviour that had meaning and it was important to find out what that meaning might be. I then carried out an analysis of the observations that I had done. These were two hours each, so six hours altogether, of continuous observation (this was before I had done the research to show that 40 minutes would be sufficient). What became clear from the observation was that all of his behaviours belonged to a much earlier stage of development than his chronological age.

I arranged a meeting with his mum to discuss his early life and to ask the key question: "Do you remember anything that happened before the age of five that was frightening for him or for you, or significant in some other way?" Mum immediately responded with, "He had a drop fit when he was ten months old and fell off my knee onto the floor". This immediately allowed me to make sense of the information that I already had. In his day-to-day behaviour, everything had to be dropped onto the floor, indicating that this was associated with a traumatic memory. It was also clear that the behaviours were repetitive and fitted into a practising stage of development, associated at its early point with a chronological age of ten months. Once we had established this as the meaning of his behaviour, we were able to put in place an intervention to help him. This involved a named person at respite who always worked with him from the moment he arrived and throughout his stay. Then, at school, he had two teaching assistants who worked with him all the time, with one of them taking the lead and the other providing support. At home he had his mum as his key significant other. Within a very short time he responded well to this intervention. Initially, I had asked the staff if they could carry him so that he would feel safe and protected. They were reluctant at first as he was known to be able to pinch the back of your neck and this could be painful. However, when they understood the meaning and the reason, they agreed to try it. I was confident that he would not need to be carried for very long and this proved to be the case. He very quickly wriggled to get down and was happy to hold hands, so long as he remained in contact with his safety person. It was quite dramatic to see the instant change in his distress and his ability to be with people.

Freddie had a known brain condition that meant he would deteriorate over time and this had influenced thinking about the possible reason for his very difficult behaviour. When we addressed his emotional developmental stage, and put in place the intervention described above, it became clear that his difficulty related more to his emotional trauma than to his primary condition. Addressing that emotional trauma by providing him with the emotional support that he needed made a huge difference to his life, and to the lives of his family. I had already speculated on the impact of addressing trauma on cognitive ability, and Freddie proved to be an excellent example of this. He had not been able to take much part in his educational opportunities because of his distress, but once he was able to feel safe and relate to the adults around him, he began to learn. Within a very short time, probably only one term of the school year, he had progressed to the next class, and within a year had progressed to the top-class. He still had the difficulties of his primary condition, which included limited language, but he was able to show through his response to learning opportunities that he could access his cognitive ability much better.

This was my first example of working indirectly with an individual, as opposed to individual psychotherapy. It was possible to get the staff team and the family to engage in the work because they were in a state of desperation with such a distressed child. It did become necessary to provide him with a safe space at home because there were other children and mum couldn't always be there for him. So he had a safe space at home which he adopted as a happy place and he was happy to be there by himself when his mum was busy. The room was fitted out with padding and sensory stimulation so that it could be a happy place. This sort of provision has been found to be useful in other cases, so long as it is used positively and not as a seclusion facility. I was very impressed with the willingness and enthusiasm with which the school staff and the respite care staff engaged with the process. Everyone was distressed by Freddie's behaviour and could see that it wasn't him wishing to harm other people, but more an expression of distress that could be understood.

We can understand and accept that, at the time of the drop fit, the emphasis would be on trying to understand why he was having seizures and what needed to be done about that. The response generally to this sort of event is a practical medical examination and response. It was only because of my own interest in early trauma that we were able to discover the difficulty. It was notable, as well, that one of Freddie's other behaviours had been a tendency to hide under a giant teddy bear, thereby shutting out the world. This being recognised later as an escape behaviour, which he engaged in when everything was too stressful. During the initial exploration of the meaning of his behaviour, I did see him for a couple of individual sessions. In the first one he cleared every surface in the room of its contents, with everything ending up on the floor. In the second session, after we had put in place the intervention and support, he was able to sit and look at me, and play with the toys that I had taken to the session. It was a very moving experience, both to recognise the pain that this little boy had been experiencing, and to accept that something therapeutic could be done for him.

Chapter 7: Annie and Jackie

This is a slightly different look at intervention for two people working together.

I want to look now at a slightly different example, but one based on the same theoretical underpinnings. I first met Annie and Jackie when Annie was referred. Her behaviour at the time involved lots of inappropriate actions in public places, including shouting, swearing and generally disruptive behaviour. She was known to have an intellectual disability and was still living at home, and her family were struggling and hoping that she would be able to be accommodated by statutory services. She had formed a friendship with Jackie, who was already known to services as someone in need of support. However, neither of them met the criteria for a full support package from social services or health. They were regular attenders at A&E, with overdose attempts, various physical ailments, sometimes as a result of fighting, and both were known as highly disruptive individuals.

When I was first asked to see them from a psychological point of view, there was hope and expectation that I would be able to understand their behaviour and offer some therapeutic support that might enable them to change. I met with them together and separately, and established that they both came from quite troubled backgrounds with a lot of traumatic experiences in their early lives. This was in the early days of the recognition of emotional developmental delay in response to trauma, before the FAIT had been developed. My assessment of their emotional developmental stage was that Annie was very definitely at the practising stage, with lots of repetitive behaviours and destructive patterns that she seemed unable to break. Jackie, however, was into the rapprochement stage and was able to at least consider another person's point of view. Neither were fully individuated, and therefore not able to manage their own lives without support. Neither of them had safe and effective family support, and both were, to some extent, exploited by their families as they both had access to disability allowances enabling them to have some financial independence, but it was money that others coveted.

My role in their lives became quite mixed. It was clearly essential that they had some sort of safe base and, at that time, the local housing department had quite a number of empty flats so were able to offer them housing. Their behaviour, as neighbours, was not always acceptable and, in the time that I knew them, they moved three times. Fortunately, as mentioned above, there was plenty of housing available and their moves did not cause any serious problem. As they progressed in terms of their understanding of their trauma, with a combination of positive support and some therapy, they settled and, at the time of me moving from their service, they had been settled in their flat for 18 months. They had also acquired a cat and were looking after it properly. They had established better relationships with their families, with clear boundaries over finances and other things.

In terms of their trauma and emotional development, it had become possible to put in place positive support from health and social teams that enabled them to develop a stronger sense of self and a better understanding of where they fitted in relation to other people. The fact that Jackie was a little bit further forward in her emotional development meant that she was able to support Annie and together they moved forward to a good rapprochement relationship with each other. This was my first example of an intervention that worked primarily without professional support. Clearly, the professional understanding of the relationship and the difficulties of relating to other people had played a big role in helping them to become more settled and more aware of their difficulties. They came to accept that they couldn't change what had happened in their early lives, but to take what responsibility they could for their present and future lives. Both had a degree of intellectual disability, with Annie's more severe than Jackie's, but, with positive encouragement and recognition of the meaning of their behaviour, it became possible to enable them to live a relatively ordinary life.

Had we not reached an understanding of the meaning of their behaviour, Jackie would almost certainly have ended up with a diagnosis of 'personality disorder', and possibly been detained at some point as her behaviour could become quite antisocial. Similarly, Annie, with a more pronounced intellectual disability, would almost certainly have ended up in residential care, or even a secure environment as her behaviour in public could at times be extreme. By enabling them to live together, and having a very helpful housing officer who recognised their need to move from time to time, it was possible for them to move on from their primary trauma, to process relationship difficulties, to resist pressure from their families, and to form a healthy emotional bond with each other.

These two ladies effectively became each other's significant other. It has been possible to replicate these findings with other duos since then. It does need to be remembered that we can't consider another person until our own sense of security is strong enough. This wouldn't have worked if neither of them had reached rapprochement. After a couple of years, they were both securely in late rapprochement and able to function as a working pair. Sometimes, this involves a romantic relationship and at other times they are friends. That is irrelevant to the overall quality of their lives, where meaningful human interaction is the key to emotional security.

Chapter 8: Brian

In this chapter, we consider what we can do when a condition has been missed for many years.

This story is about an older man, in his 60s at the time of writing. He's someone I've known for nearly 20 years and his early history is very distressing. This gentleman doesn't use verbal language at all, but will use his own adaptation of Makaton signs and actively tries to communicate with people. We have considered over the years that he probably can read and does in fact understand a great deal of what is going on around him. However, he does have a moderate intellectual disability and that has been known since he was a child, together with his mutism.

There is no doubt that this older man is still responding to traumatic experiences he had as a child. He is very destructive and can be aggressive towards his environment in the form of urinating and occasionally defecating where he shouldn't. When we did the initial Frankish assessment, we worked out that the majority of his behaviours came into the practising range, with some early rapprochement behaviours, but with these being primarily to get something that he wants. It became clear that he does have some understanding that other people can meet his needs, which is clearly a rapprochement behaviour.

In the early stages of trying to help him to live a more ordinary life and to have some satisfaction and fun in life, we did our best to understand the meaning of his behaviour. We always start from a position that all behaviour has meaning, that it all comes from somewhere. It follows that there is a category of behaviour which the Frankish assessment identifies, and then there are the specific behaviours that relate usually to traumatic life experiences. From the recognition of these two factors, we came to an understanding that the trauma, at least the initial trauma, occurred when Brian was less than two years old. But what we also know is that people are traumatised again and again when their initial trauma is not recognised. It means that every time someone tries to communicate with Brian at an age-appropriate level, the mismatch between his physical age and his emotional age means that those communications can be viewed as hostile, over demanding, or just not understood. If we imagine saying to an 18-month-old child that they need to get ready because it's time to go out they wouldn't know where to begin. They would wait for you to get them ready. They wouldn't know where their clothes were, where their shoes were, maybe even what 'going out' meant. Having a whole lifetime of this mismatch leads to extreme anxiety and usually an acting out of that anxiety. What Brian does is break something. This distracts everyone from whatever the demand was, shows everyone how distressed he is, and diverts attention to having to mend what's been broken instead of doing whatever was planned. This may lead to some negative comments, to other people being denied an outing, to yet more expense and interruption as repairs are carried out. If the destruction involves water leaks, which it may do if radiators are pulled off walls, then there is usually a major upheaval.

It is possible, and perhaps usual, to think of this destructive behaviour as a direct attack on the care facility or the people providing the support. It is not uncommon for people who display such behaviour to be moved into more robust environments, often in a secure setting. If the behaviour is seen as deliberate, planned in some way, or not understood at all, then the possibility of an inappropriate placement becomes more likely. It's not easy to recognise the behaviour as a response to something that happened in the past. We begin to think about what might have happened in the past to lead to such an expression of distress. It is important to recognise the behaviour as distressed behaviour, not deliberately destructive, otherwise there is a tendency to retaliate with restrictive practices.

What has become clear over the years that we have worked with Brian, as we have analysed his behaviour from the point of view of emotional disability, is that, as a young child, when his family couldn't work out what his behaviour meant or manage it, or receive the right level of support to help them, he was often locked in a bedroom, and sometimes in a cupboard. He has a fear of small spaces and of being shut in. This is very distressing to think about, as the assessment shows that this experience relates to his life as a very young child. There are some other behaviours that indicate physical and sexual abuse. This is again very difficult for support staff to know and to work with. What we find is that by asking support staff to provide emotional support appropriate to the emotional age, we can establish positive ways of working. They don't need to know all the bad things that have happened, they just need to know that bad things did happen, and that his behaviour now is a consequence of those things. What we also need to know, and the evidence base is growing, is that providing the appropriate emotional support leads to emotional growth. By providing the right level of input, for example by accepting what he can't do because he doesn't understand why he should do it, we can avoid conflict, at least some of the time. No one gets it right all the time, nor do parents in the support provided to their children. When they have a child with an intellectual disability, they are very dependent on professional support and advice which is not always available. What we do know is that professional support and advice on emotional development is, more often than not, not available. One of the reasons for telling these stories is to try and change that.

Brian was provided with his own space, bedroom, bathroom, kitchen and living room. He became a collector of mechanical toys, mostly stored in boxes and rarely played with, but they became important to him as his possessions. It seems to be important to him to have things that are his, which is another indicator of deprivation in early childhood. We suspect that he had very few if any toys as a youngster. Over the years, there has been quite long periods of quite settled behaviour during which Brian has felt in tune with his support staff, he has engaged with lots of activities and outings and holidays, and has responded well. His emotional developmental stage moved into being primarily early rapprochement and with some late rapprochement behaviours coming into play as he clearly set about negotiating for things he wanted. His discrimination skills increased and he learned to work out what he could get from different staff at different times. His interaction with people who lived in neighbouring flats improved.

Sadly, Brian developed diabetes and was not able to easily comply with the dietary restrictions. One of his long-standing behaviours had been taking food that wasn't necessarily his, indicating fear of not being fed. This had got much better, but the restrictions required to manage the diabetes led to more clashes with staff. It proved quite difficult to get the right support from health colleagues for a gentleman with moderate intellectual disabilities and distressed behaviour who needed specialist support for his diabetes. As a consequence, the diabetes was not as well-regulated as it could have been. Brian then began to show other behaviours that were new, notably hitting out at other people and becoming quite frightening. We speculated about whether this was a completely new behaviour, related to the diabetes, early-onset dementia, or an activation of a past trauma. If the latter, then it would seem to link with food and food deprivation. If he had experience of food deprivation as a young child but had come to trust that his support environment would make sure he was never without food, he could have become traumatised again by the restrictions on food imposed as a consequence of his diabetes.

The regression to practising behaviours continued to differentiation behaviours, where almost everything became self-referenced. This meant that his support package needed to give him everything he needed like a very young child, and could not expect anything of him that he couldn't deliver. This was very sad for the people who had supported him for many years and helped him to become established at the rapprochement stage, able to work with others, able to contribute to groups and group activities.

It was not clear if the deterioration, physical and emotional, was or is caused by the physical condition, or the impact of the physical condition on activating past trauma. It does seem at least likely that it is reactivation of past trauma that has led to the distress and the expression of anger and despair. However, it is extremely helpful to assess his behaviour in relation to the stages of emotional development, and to provide the support and care that matches the present state.

If we were to use a medical model, we would be inclined to provide education, both for the diabetes and for the emotional distress. If we were to use a behavioural model, we would be likely to ignore the distressed behaviour and work with him when he wasn't showing difficult behaviour. But with a trauma informed model we are recognising the meaning of the behaviour and working at an emotional level that matches. The intention is to reduce the distress and anxiety he experiences, increase his sense of peace, and provide a safe living environment for him and others.

Chapter 9: Kevin

In this chapter we consider the impact of sibling influence and more extreme behaviour in response to individual trauma.

Kevin is a young man with a complicated and traumatic history. This has left him in a situation where he needs constant support in order to lead a relatively ordinary life. Were he not provided with the level of support that he needs, he would be likely to be in secure services in segregation.

Kevin is autistic and has a moderate intellectual disability. He has a younger brother who is a high achiever. A study of his history and present behaviour, assessed using the FAIT, would indicate that one of his traumatic life events was his younger brother overtaking him in education terms. Prior to that happening, despite some difficulties, the family were able to provide him with what he needed. He attended special school and seemed quite happy there. There were then changes at the school which happened to correspond, we think, with his realisation that his younger brother was overtaking him in terms of academic achievement. These changes at the school resulted in a lower level of individual support. The assessment of his emotional developmental age would indicate the need for 24-hour emotional support, i.e. knowing who was there for him at all times. This is of course hard for schools to accept when they have a child who has been functioning quite well at their level of ability, and then suddenly doesn't. It requires an understanding of the difference and interaction between emotional and cognitive disability. Sadly, once the safe relationship has been lost, it takes some time to re-establish. When I first became involved with Kevin, he was very distressed, very destructive, and quite unresponsive to attempts to help him. His parents and younger brother were coping with significant disruption at home, including broken televisions and suchlike within the home.

The usual multidisciplinary response to someone with this presentation is to consider medication, residential school, moving towards a restricted environment. Kevin's parents were struggling with this as a way forward, and were looking for an alternative approach. They responded well to a formulation that included an emotional developmental delay. They could recognise events in the family history that could have contributed to

Kevin's distress. They were, however, concerned about the range of options open to them as a family, and Kevin specifically.

An attempt was made to establish a therapeutic relationship with individual sessions. It became clear from the sessions that Kevin was cognitively more able than was obvious from his presentation. It was also clear that he was hypervigilant, indicating fear and anxiety. This led to more exploration about what was concerning him. However, when considering that his behaviours were indicative of an emotional developmental stage at the practising level, it became more obvious that he would be insecure and anxious if he didn't know who was making the world safe at that moment in time. What became clear was that he worked better with some people than others, showing clear signs of discrimination and different levels of emotional security and safety. This was helpful in identifying a pattern of work with him, supporting him emotionally, and helping the staff to access his cognitive ability. The thinking behind this approach is, again, as with the other people described in this book, that, if we provide an emotionally nurturing environment, further development can happen. It follows that the interruption in emotional development is not fixed, it is fluid, and, subject to the right intervention, can progress. What we wanted to see with Kevin was that he could progress to the early rapprochement stage and become able to recognise the role of the people in his life and two-way interaction that felt safe and more equal. It was clear that he reacted badly to people taking charge and telling him what to do. As he was now a big, strong teenager, it was important to help him to develop sufficiently emotionally to be able to work together with those trying to support him. To do this he needed to be provided with an emotionally nurturing environment that matched his emotional developmental stage. At the beginning of the work, this was equivalent to a 10 to 15-month-old child.

It is quite hard for families, school staff and social care support staff to accept that a mischievous and strong young man can be functioning as a toddler. But if this can be accepted, and everyone can provide the secure emotional environment that is needed, then progress can be made. It may be necessary to use occasional medication if things get out of hand. With the child who is naturally at that stage, we would pick them up and take them for a nap, or pop them in a pushchair and take them for a walk. Clearly, you cannot do that with the six-foot, 12-stone young man. Therefore, the emphasis is on preventing tantrums by providing emotional input and support, together with suitable activities and cognitive stimulation. This requires a lot of forethought and planning, and, inevitably, can't work all the time. It just needs the phone to ring, or someone to knock on the door, or the TV not to work, or the key member of staff or parent needing to go to the bathroom, and the pattern is lost. Work needs to go into planning the pattern to the finest detail as possible, with contingency plans in place. With Kevin, it was clear that he needed more than one person with him to provide an appropriate level of emotional security. It was important, however, that at any moment in time, it was clear which person was 'his' person. This allows them to swap for relief, and to make sure that Kevin became more flexible in accepting that, so long as he knew who it was that was looking after him at that moment in time, he could manage.

It was difficult to get everyone to understand and accept what was needed and what could be funded. It is extremely important to recognise that the extra expense of providing this type of support does lead to saving the cost of a secure residential placement that might be needed if progress in emotional development doesn't happen. It is hoped that, over time, the arresting of emotional development will be recognised much earlier and interventions put in place much earlier, and that these will not be so intense or so expensive.

Let's go back to the beginning of this young man's life. He was born into an ordinary family who had no idea about what autism was or what impact it was going to have on their lives. They had a second child before anyone really recognised the level of their first child's needs. Kevin had several fairly ordinary childhood experiences of hospital and minor illnesses that may have had a bigger impact on him because of his atypical response to events. However, in the early stages, he was able to travel with his parents, go on holidays, go to school and to manage. There would be no obvious signs to the parents that he was experiencing an interruption in his emotional development.

What happens with youngsters who have got stuck in their emotional development is that they experience new events as traumatic because they are not secure enough in their own identity to be able to tolerate things that change around them. Hence, they respond by either withdrawing or distressed behaviour which becomes a challenge to those providing care. Repetitive behaviours are seen in autism and become accepted to some extent. Repetitive behaviours that belong to the practising stage of emotional development are a passing phase and need to be recognised as such. Then, interventions and activities need to be in place to facilitate development to the next stage. If it is assumed that the repetitive behaviour is purely autism, it will be accepted rather than used in the progression of the emotional self. Sadly, families do not generally get this sort of information from professionals at the time it is needed. This is partly because they don't come to the attention of the professionals, and partly because most professionals in young children's services are taught to concentrate on physical and cognitive development, only considering social development at a later stage. However, a child who is delayed in their emotional development will not progress in their social development, and by the time it is recognised, will have already lost several years of development.

Kevin was eventually provided with an excellent education opportunity and formed a trusting relationship with his tutor, such that he could hold on to his relationship even when the tutor was not present. This was real progress, representative of further emotional development. Piaget spoke many years ago about object permanence and that the ability to hold another in mind when they are not present is linked to a developing sense of self.

Chapter 10: Jane

Here, we consider how commissioned services can provide a solution to the distress caused by emotional abuse.

I'm going to talk about a young lady, Jane, who has a mild intellectual disability and a history of abuse and neglect. When I first met her, it was clear that she had good spoken language and a number of life skills, but was hindered specifically in her social relationships. She was also at risk of harm from family members and people who knew her in the area where she lived. A decision was made to move her away to another area where she was unknown and considerably safer. At first, she reacted badly to being moved from people that she knew, while at the same time she began to feel pleased to be safe. Although she was in her 30s, an assessment of her emotional developmental stage indicated that she was functioning at the practising level.

When faced with an adult with such severe emotional developmental delay, there is inevitably a question of why. When Jane was referred to us, there was not a huge amount of information available, but it became clear that treatment within her family had been less than ideal. We speculated about the possibility that all of her difficulties had been blamed on her cognitive impairment and intellectual disability. Neither family nor professionals seemed to be able to recognise the impact that early trauma had had on her emotional development. The FAIT assessment indicated that she was at the practising stage, so her support plans included the safe significant other and lots of low-demand, repetitive activities. Over time she began to relax and trust others and developed two-way rapprochement behaviours.

Jane settled into her new environment and began to benefit from the input of trained and supportive staff. Many of her behaviours were quite destructive and antisocial and needed to be understood. Her personal hygiene behaviours needed a lot of attention. This needed to be seen in the context of her delayed emotional development, the consequence of which was an inability to recognise her impact on others. The development of social skills, empathy and consideration of other people only comes with the rapprochement stage of emotional development. The challenge has been to provide Jane with the opportunity to develop those rapprochement abilities. She has responded well to the input she has received. The first and main provision has been the availability of a significant other person at all times. In her present placement, Jane has always known, and still knows, who her 'go-to' person is at all times. This has significantly reduced her anxiety and increased her self-esteem. The implication is that, in her previous life, she did not feel important enough to anyone. Knowing she is a valued human being has opened the doors for her to develop social skills, social awareness and trust, and to progress to a higher level of emotional development.

Jane has engaged with individual therapy to help her process the trauma that led to her arrested emotional development. As she was functioning as if she was still a toddler, emotionally, this inevitably involved exploring family relationships. This is always painful for people to do, as it raises questions about why the parents did not treat the person better. It is of course vital that therapists do not try to answer those social questions, but stay with the client with their memories and their distress, and help them to build a stronger sense of themselves as valued individuals. In the trauma informed care model, therapy is not always indicated, but in Jane's case, it has been an essential part of her recovery and progress.

In understanding the impact of early trauma on Jane, it has been possible to provide her with a therapeutic intervention that has enabled her to process much of what had happened to her in the past. As a consequence, she has made progress and can look forward to a more satisfying future. It is sad to think about what would have happened had she remained stuck in a traumatised state with inadequate or inappropriate support.

Her lack of progress in the past will have been because of a lack of knowledge or understanding of the underlying cause of her distressed behaviour. It can be very easy to get into studying specific difficult behaviours and coming up with a behavioural programme to try to reduce, remove or correct the behaviour. When we move away from looking at the specific behaviour, and look instead at the category of behaviours and where they fit in the emotional developmental model, we can see the approach is quite different. Using a behavioural approach of 'reward and ignore' has a negative impact on someone who is emotionally less than two years old. Their perception of the behavioural programme is that it is punitive, especially if the distressed behaviour is ignored in an attempt to reduce it. All it does is increase the despair and either lead to more distressed behaviour, or to a withdrawal from interaction. If the distressed behaviour increases, it can lead to breakdown and support package replacement. If withdrawal is a consequence, then the person's quality of life is further reduced, which is not a positive outcome.

We found with Jane that she was able to progress to the early rapprochement stage and, after a few years, made progress into the late rapprochement stage. This improved her quality of life significantly, allowing her to join in community activities and facilitating the development of friendships.

Understanding and accepting that early trauma gets missed is crucial to moving forward to a better way of supporting people who have been through the experience of early trauma. Stories like Jane's are not uncommon.

Chapter 11: Nathan and Daniel

This chapter looks at two young boys struggling to make sense of the world. They are not related but presented with similar trauma experiences.

Nathan and Daniel were both referred at the age of seven. Both were very unsettled, struggled to go to school, and both were schooled at home. They both had younger siblings. They were both very active and lively, quite strong and capable of being quite destructive and harmful to the parents, their siblings or their environment. Both sets of parents were at their wits end trying to comply with the legal requirement to get the children to school, while at the same time trying to understand why the children were so out of step with ordinary life.

Both boys had a diagnosis of intellectual disability and autism. Both were attending special school appropriately, but both struggled to attend every day. There were major difficulties with transport and Nathan's parents were transporting him themselves. Daniel's parents were not able to do this and that was a struggle every day with the school bus.

The question with both boys was, as usual, why? I spent time with both families gathering a detailed history, and gained a comprehensive picture of what life was like in the family homes. I also spent time in school observing their behaviour in the classroom and gathering information from teaching and support staff. I also completed the assessment of the impact of trauma (FAIT). From my initial observation, I had already surmised that they were not individuated, and did not have the confidence to hold onto their identity when separated from their parents, so expected that I would find delayed emotional development. This would be a further disability on top of cognitive intellectual disability and autism. Not all children with intellectual disabilities and autism have these difficulties, so there must be another element – namely, delayed emotional development.

In order to distinguish between autistic people, and autistic people with additional trauma, it seems to be very important to recognise both the similarities and the differences. This involves recognising the similarities between children with cognitive impairments, the similarities between the behaviour of one autistic child and that of another, and the difference between those who have and don't have delayed emotional development and a consequent emotional disability. Carrying out detailed observations of the boys for the assessment tool revealed that both children were delayed at the practising stage. As this relates to the ten to 15-month-old stage of neurotypical development, we looked for an event that happened at that stage to see if it made sense of why Nathan and Daniel had got stuck.

As usual, my approach was to ask the boys' families if they could think of anything that the children had reacted strongly to before the age of five. A detailed interview with the parents revealed quite quickly that the major event that had had a big effect on both children was the arrival of a younger sibling. As I have mentioned, not all children react negatively to the arrival of a sibling, but all are affected and may process the information in a way that is traumatic for them. In this case, one of the mums described noticing her son's negative facial expression when being introduced to the new baby, but she did not recognise it as the major event that it was for him. She saw very quickly that a lot of his behaviour had stayed the same from that time, but she had attributed this to his intellectual disability and autism. She had not received any professional help that might have enabled her to recognise his arrested development as an emotional response to a changed world which no longer felt as safe as it once had.

Once we had identified the traumatic experience, it was possible to put in place a therapeutic intervention that would facilitate progress from the emotional developmental stage of practicing to the next stage of early rapprochement. We know that children who have reached the rapprochement stage can reason to some extent, accept and trust explanations provided by their parents and become generally more settled and easier to help.

With Daniel, we were able to have some individual therapy sessions with him and his mum together, which led to them working together in a better way. Before this, his mum had wanted to help but didn't know how. Providing her with a model for understanding Daniel's delayed emotional development helped her to provide the secure emotional environment that he needed. This involved giving the emotional support and certainty in daily life that a one-year-old would need, perhaps for up to 18 months. Fortunately, what we have also found with this approach is that the response is quick. Once the emotional support is put in place the child responds, reacts, has a real reduction in anxiety and begins to interact positively. It took only a few weeks for Daniel to be able to go back to school. He became able to use the school bus and trust that his mum would be there when he returned. He also came to understand that the school staff could be his 'safe people' in between, named and formally transferred.

The impact of this knowledge on the way of working was dramatic for the family. Lots of things that they had been unable to do because of Daniel's behaviour and anxiety became possible. Notably, his attending school every day released his mother to work and to spend time with her other child. It is a source of distress that the professionals involved at the time of the trauma were not trained to notice it. We cannot expect parents to notice, especially when their child has a diagnosis of intellectual disability and autism, so they are expecting different things. It is extremely likely that children without intellectual disabilities and autism can be similarly traumatised, but it does not come to the attention of parents and professionals in the same way. Neurotypical children usually receive support in preparing them for the arrival of a sibling and most cope fairly well. We know, however, from adult work, that anyone can be traumatised by events that fundamentally change their lives.

If we turn now to Nathan, one of his distressing behaviours was biting. This was distressing, of course, for his family and for the children and staff at school. He needed to be excluded from quite a lot of group activities. He had to be extremely well supervised at home to make sure he didn't bite his younger brother. An observation of his behaviour showed, again, that he was still emotionally at the practicing stage. His behaviours were repetitive and not goal-oriented. He did what he knew how to do and repeated these behaviours.

When we looked into his early history to try and understand why biting had become one of his repetitive behaviours, we quickly discovered that feeding had been a major problem for him as a baby. His mother had suffered from postnatal depression and had struggled to be there for him. This, almost inevitably, led to his mother feeling bad about what she had not been able to do. This increased anxiety in both mother and child. The arrival of a second child increased this anxiety further, as Nathan's mum was afraid that the same thing might happen. It didn't, but the impact on Nathan of the arrival of the second child was significant. He already had a diagnosis of intellectual disability and autism so it was, again, almost inevitably accepted that his deterioration in behaviour was related to those conditions. And again, professionals did not recognise the impact of trauma on the consequent interruption to his emotional development, accepting that his behaviour was almost to be accepted or expected because of his known difficulties. Sadly, because the behaviour was biting, it was very serious and this led to Nathan being quite restricted. He also had great difficulty sleeping and this put an enormous strain on the family as well.

Nathan was attending school and travelling on the school bus. We put in place a system whereby he always had a known significant other person available to him. His mum would hand him over to the person providing safety on the bus, and this person would hand him over formally to the teaching assistant when he arrived at school. While at school, he would have a named person to whom he knew he could go to receive the relevant emotional support. This effectively provided him with a significant other safe person all the time. This is a requirement in the process of facilitating development to the next stage. Fortunately, Nathan attached very well to a teaching assistant at the school. He was also very emotionally attached to his dad. It was possible to ensure that the bus escort was the same person, so collectively he had a small group that formed his emotional support network. Nathan responded well to this intervention and became able to work together with people, moving into the early rapprochement stage of emotional development. He stopped biting, started learning, and showed both an increase in his emotional developmental stage and his cognitive ability.

He was, however, still very anxious and he was prescribed some medication to try and help him to be more relaxed. It was clear when working with him that his heart rate was always very high, and it was felt that this was not good for him in the long term. He initially responded well to the medication, but then started to react to it and it had to be withdrawn. However, by this time, the people working with him, including his parents, had gained more skills in providing a safe emotional environment. He did quite well for a couple of years but then, sadly, his mother struggled to accept him and her own anxiety about the difficulties they had faced when he was born became overwhelming. This led to more difficulties, and he was eventually moved into alternative care.

What these two cases illustrate is that change can happen and it can happen quite quickly if the correct intervention is put in place, following from a correct identification of the difficulty. For both of these boys, it would have been better if the trauma had been noticed at the time that it happened. That's probably true of everyone. What we do know is that traumatised children are further traumatised by events that are quite ordinary to other people but are experienced by the individual from that position of emotional disability, so in fact, create further trauma. There is a strong argument for early identification. Most developmental assessments concentrate on physical skills and, to some extent, social skills, but do not generally pick up on the subtleties of emotional developmental delay. There is no doubt that some of this is because of the lowered expectations of the child that is already identified as learning disabled. It is hoped that emotional development, and emotional disability will become part of the mainstream assessment of all children. It may be that children with intellectual disabilities and autism, who have an additional emotional disability, can be helped at an earlier stage. This would lead, almost certainly, to less family breakdowns, less distressed behaviour, and less institutional care.

Chapter 12: Mary

Does being more disabled protect us from trauma or make it even harder to process?

I'm going to talk now about somebody with a more severe cognitive impairment. People with less cognitive ability seem to be labelled as behaviourally disturbed because of that cognitive impairment. I hypothesise that the main difficulty is the emotional development that hasn't occurred, influenced by the cognitive impairment, but influenced more by the treatment they receive because of the cognitive impairment. If you go into a classroom in a special school for more profoundly disabled people, there is often an atmosphere around doing things, for example changing, feeding, turning to make comfortable, and other physical tasks. Because there is usually little or no language, there is very little exploration of feelings. In addition, it is extremely painful, sometimes, for staff to witness the level of disability. This is made worse by the individuals not being able to say what is distressing them when they cry. Inevitably, the distressed behaviour can include aggressive behaviour towards staff, other children, or themselves. It is extremely distressing for staff to work with people who are injuring themselves. The pain that the disabled individual inflicts on themselves must be an indicator of how distressed they are. They can't tell you what is distressing them. Our task is to try and identify what that might be. The assessment of the emotional developmental stage is a crucial part of the process.

It can be quite hard to sit in a therapeutic space with someone who doesn't speak, but it is amazing to experience the projections of feeling that become available once the therapeutic space is established. I have spent many hours engaged in such activity, being willing and open to any message that the person attempted to communicate. Sometimes the feelings of sadness and depression are very intense, and it becomes understandable that staff working 13-hour shifts cannot engage at that level because it becomes intolerable. This adds further weight to the argument for a holistic approach and providing emotional security as a team effort. Individual therapy may be needed as well, but sometimes it isn't.

Thinking about Mary and her history helps us to understand her behaviour and approaches that have helped her. She was born to parents who had limited cognitive ability themselves. They couldn't manage a baby and they injured her, leading to her going into the care at the age of approximately 12 months. I don't have the full history of what was provided at that time, but by the time I met Mary and carried out an assessment of her emotional disability, it was clear that, emotionally, she had not moved on from the 12-month stage.

If we consider her experience as being emotionally 12 months old, cognitively higher but severely disabled, and with no family support, we might reasonably expect problems. Mary had periods of her life where she was restrained, secluded, heavily medicated, and led a very restricted life. This was inevitably further traumatising for her. People caring for her became frustrated because she couldn't seem to appreciate anything they did for her. This led to them being further withdrawn from her, leaving her isolated and further emotionally deprived.

Mary was fostered for a while as a child, but her foster carers would not have been given information about her emotional needs. She was a young girl with a severe intellectual disability and the concentration would have been on trying to develop her skills, possibly her language, and her cognitive rather than emotional development. It was commonly believed that people with severe intellectual disabilities did not share the same sorts of feelings as others, almost certainly because it was too painful to realise how sad they might be. The sadness and unhappiness would be a direct response to feeling unseen, unheard and unloved.

As time went on, Mary became an NHS patient in long-term care. Over quite a long period, maybe ten to 15 years, her world became smaller and she became more isolated. She was unable to share a living space with anyone else and ended up having a whole unit to herself. Attempts to interact with her were met with rejection, screaming, and sometimes physical attacks, including biting. All of these behaviours could be seen as normal for a one-year-old, but not for a fully grown woman. There were times when she was secluded because the behaviour couldn't be managed. Medication levels went above safe BNF limits in a desperate attempt to help her calm down. There is no doubt the people providing services for her wanted to make it better. However, her carers were unfamiliar with the ideas of emotional disability, and mostly trained to use behavioural approaches and medication to manage behaviour. Behavioural approaches require that the person whose behaviour is being modified can value the approval or disapproval of the person who is there. They also require an interest in new activities.

Eventually, Mary was provided with a social care environment in a single-person service. Having been assessed as emotionally at the practicing stage (around ten to 15 months), it was possible to put in place the right staffing, with the presence at all times of a significant other to keep the world safe, be reliable and provide the equivalent of the primary carer or parent. This meant that Mary always knew who was there for her, who could meet her needs for food, personal care or play. This led to a reduction in anxiety and an increase in her ability to take notice of other people and not be so emotionally isolated. However, after so many years of traumatic 'care', it took time for her to trust that the world would be safe, that she would always have what she needed, and that life could be fun. There were times, and no doubt still are, when she was not able to manage her feelings and would regress to the screaming baby tantrum stage. In the past, this had been responded to with restraint and seclusion. This was changed to the provision of a safe room, the equivalent of a cot or pram, where she could go until she calmed down. The safe room in situations like this needs to be a three-quarter door with the staff staying in contact, soothing music and lights like a sensory room, and, of course, full padding to avoid injury. Mary quickly became able to use the safe room, choosing herself to use it at times, and other times needing to be guided into the room. Restraint didn't happen at all, and this was of benefit to everyone, allowing for relational security through the meeting of emotional needs instead of imposed physical security with the use of overpowering control.

There are several people like Mary in segregated provision in NHS and private provision across the country. Many of them were independently reviewed in 2021 or thereabouts. The ones that I reviewed all fitted into the same pattern as has been described here for Mary. They were all subject to restraint and seclusion, heavy medication, and a lack of understanding of their emotional needs. This puts an enormous strain on the staff as well as on the individuals themselves. In some cases, it was possible to provide information about emotional developmental delay and the success of programmes that have been achieved, leading to a willingness to try a different approach.

The most pressing issue is the need to recognise arrested emotional development earlier. If, as has been described in other chapters, the difficulty can be recognised in childhood, there is every possibility of avoiding further trauma and further regression or stunting of development. Another positive that has been found is that, if the emotional need is met and emotional development progresses, there is a corresponding progress in cognitive ability. It is as though the reduction in anxiety and the acceptance of self frees up the part of the brain that can think. That is a real benefit to people who have limited thinking ability anyway, but can access what they have. If emotional development progresses into the early rapprochement stage, then the quality of relationships improves enormously.

I would like to see a situation where there were no more Marys in the world. Where everyone who needs additional emotional support to develop and grow into their true self can have that. In the meantime, it is hoped that adults who are stuck in this situation will get the care they deserve and need. And that infant mental health and preschool provision will recognise the people who need this approach and provide it much earlier.

Chapter 13: Robert

Can we come to a better understanding of self-harming behaviours?

We come on now to a young man with a long history of failed placements and a lack of understanding of his basic emotional needs. We will call him Robert. There is a long history of abuse within the family, physical and emotional, rather than sexual. The behaviour described as the most distressing and least understood is headbanging. He will spend long periods banging his forehead against a wall or a bedhead or a cupboard, often leaving wounds.

Valerie Sinason talks about headbanging as a response to unbearable thoughts. This is almost certainly relevant in Robert's case but is a condition that many people in professional roles find equally unbearable and therefore difficult to address and manage. Robert has limited spoken language, coupled with an extreme loyalty to his family, and, when we encountered him was unable to talk freely about the thoughts that were troubling him. Sitting with him in a therapy setting enabled me to connect to his pain. He was always very quick to distract my attention with activities or toys, avoiding facing up to the issues of his internal pain. This was clearly a defence against the pain and an unconscious awareness that his pain was unbearable for the people around him. He had had many different placements and was aware that people found him very difficult to cope with.

It does seem that situations like Robert's lead to much labelling of challenging behaviour because it challenges the services that are trying to provide. As has been mentioned elsewhere, if the behaviour is referred to as distressed behaviour, we can begin to think more kindly and positively about possible interventions. It requires support for staff as well as for the individual. This is a reminder that trauma informed care has the four ingredients of a safe place to live, enough staff to support, for those staff to be supported, and individual therapy. If we can cross that barrier between our own distress at seeing someone injure themselves and the internal processing that is going on, but not in a therapeutic way, then we can begin to be helpful.

It was clear from the moment I first met Robert that he had had many years of not being understood, of people being unable to tolerate his distress, and of behavioural approaches being used to try and stop him from self-harming through headbanging.

When we came to look at Robert's emotional development and contemplate the possibility of arrested emotional development and a consequent difficulty in processing information relevant to two-way interaction, we found that we had a way forward. His behaviour could be seen to belong to the practicing stage of development, where he was engaging in behaviours that were available to him, without being able to move on to more mature interactive behaviours. It follows that there were two factors at work, one being the unbearable thoughts that relate to past events, and the other indicating the age at which the events happened which led to the unbearable thoughts.

In trauma informed care, all staff must be trained and supported to cope with a person's projected distress, and in Robert's case this was not provided until a few years ago and he continued to bang his head. Sadly, this can still happen in the event that either new staff, or existing staff, temporarily forgot that their role is to provide emotional security for him at all times.

In the early stages of his placement his head banging looked like differentiation, relating only to himself. Over time this became more conscious and took on the practising pattern. What has been found, over the time that he has been in a supportive living service with people trained to meet his needs, is that this has become a means of communicating a need, showing that he has made progress to the early rapprochement stage of emotional development. He can now ask for things that he wants, and tell people when he is upset, and it is possible to see him grow in stature as he has become more emotionally secure. But after many years of inappropriate care, his prospects of full recovery are perhaps limited. He does respond well to individual therapeutic time, but this is not funded over long periods of time. His service provider has been able to access trainees who are looking for therapy experience and to come as a free service in exchange for supervision, and this has helped. Robert has benefited from the opportunity to test out his thoughts and feelings within the safety of a therapeutic relationship and this has helped. He doesn't talk about what happened to him very much but he is able to show through drawings and the way that he engages in two-way interaction what happened to him. It is clear that he was treated as a 'nonperson' for much of his early life and was not valued as the person that he is.

The issue of being a nonperson crops up again and again in this work with emotionally traumatised people. If we reflect on the long-stay hospital provision that was common from Victorian times up to the 1980s, we can remember that people were depersonalised. I remember a story my mother told me many years ago of her being told to put 20 young men from her ward onto a bus to send them to another hospital. None of them could speak and no staff went with them. They were told to write their names on their bodies with gentian violet. I find this treatment horrendous, but at least they did what they could to try and give the young men some identity. It does help us to reflect on how painful it is to work with people who have become non-people. The projections of fear, anger pain and despair are hard to tolerate. This does to some extent explain why single-person services are both necessary and more tolerable for some clients. As soon as you put a group of people together who all have trauma in their background, the amount of pain rolling around the room becomes intolerable, and the response becomes inhumane. We have seen this happen time and again in services that are not taking into consideration the emotional issues of the people they are caring for. Recent scandals illustrate this phenomenon.

If we come back to Robert, we can see that he falls to some extent between the old institutional care and fully planned life experiences that accommodate his trauma and his present needs. His service provider recognises his needs and does its best to meet them. However, his funding organisation do not necessarily recognise all of his needs, nor can they afford to provide everything that he needs, but a near approximation is funded and he is making progress towards a more positive and effective self. Although the headbanging does still happen, there has been a reduction and it can now be recognised why it happens, when it happens.

We need always to take into account the de-synchrony between physical, cognitive and emotional development. If they are all in tune with each other then usually all is well and fortunately most of the people we know come into this category. We'll come later to think about people who have severe physical difficulties but if we stay, for the moment, with people like Robert who have a cognitive impairment, there is already de-synchrony between his physical development, which is neurotypical, and his intellectual development which is impaired. If that was all the difficulty he faced, then his life would be relatively straightforward and there would be no headbanging. But he was clearly traumatised as a very young child and he has emotional impairment as well, which is out of synchrony with both his physical and cognitive development. As has been mentioned in previous chapters, if the emotional need is met, there is a consequent improvement in cognitive ability and the availability of thoughts to the person. Instead of going round and round in circles of emotional pain leading to headbanging to try and remove thoughts, there is progress towards being able to process thoughts with the help of another person. Once there is clear interaction and recognition of support from another person, there is evidence of emotional development and growth. It is good to know that Robert has had this opportunity and is now more able to benefit from the life experiences that he is offered, to make choices, and to have confidence in the fact that he will be supported when he has a bad day and not be rejected.

Chapter 14: Miranda

A traumatised family can be more painful and hinder a positive approach.

This chapter tells the story of a traumatised family and the impact this trauma had on each member of the family. Miranda was at the centre and has a mild intellectual disability, which led to the events of the initial trauma. At the time that I met Miranda, she was in her 30s and living in a supportive living environment and had staff with her at all times. Her parents had separated but were both very involved in supporting her in her own home. However, there was constant tension between them and the support provider and the commissioners of the service. This tension, and the way that it was worked out and through, was creating further trauma and more distress for Miranda.

Families with a child with a disability are faced with lots of decisions and don't necessarily receive the best advice. People responsible for providing services for children with disabilities are often focused on educational achievement and placement, physical development and social development. They may not be skilled in assessing the emotional impact of the solutions that they offer for the educational development of those in their care. One of the decisions that was made for Miranda as a young child was that she would benefit from a residential educational placement and this was arranged for her. No one could have known at that time, because it was not widely known, that Miranda was not emotionally secure enough to be able to leave her parents and go to a residential educational placement. Everyone's intentions were motivated by a desire to find the best alternative for her. Sadly, this proved not to be a placement that could meet her emotional needs. She did very well educationally and made progress in her learning, within her capabilities. However, she was not successful in forming relationships and became vulnerable to abuse.

Because Miranda needed a safe, significant person at all times – this being the consequence of her emotional developmental delay – she was inclined to seek out support from people who weren't necessarily safe. As a consequence, she suffered some abusive experiences that she was not able to fully describe to others, so the perpetrators were not apprehended. This was traumatic for Miranda, and also for her parents who were overcome by guilt and grief. They became quite obsessive about finding the right support and therapy for their child, but were not able to process their own feelings well enough to enable them to be effective in their search.

Miranda developed ways of interacting with people that kept them involved with her, but this became quite a strain for them, leading to a high turnover of staff. As Miranda's core need was constancy and reliability, this worked against her development and improvement. At times, Miranda became very angry and distressed. But her more frequent behaviour was to become repetitive and obsessive. Using the emotional developmental model, it was clear that these behaviours fit into the practicing stage of development, belonging to the toddler stage of emotional development. However, she was physically age-appropriate and cognitively able to talk, to write and, to some extent, to read. She was clearly much more able than her emotional self could allow her to be. As she frequently had staff who didn't know her, they would inevitably respond to her cognitive self and be confused by her emotional needs and demands. Demands is a good word, because she did become very demanding and this behaviour was very much reminiscent of a toddler stamping their foot and demanding attention all the time. Staff who could recognise what was happening would respond accordingly, giving her reassurance about what was coming next, and being there to meet her needs as they arose.

An attempt was made to offer a therapeutic intervention for Miranda but this could not be provided by the available professional staff. As a consequence, she made very little progress in her development. Attempts were also made to offer support to the parents, to try and help them to live with what they couldn't change, and to support Miranda into a service that could meet her needs. Sadly, all of them had become locked into a maladaptive way of responding to the past trauma and little progress was made.

If we examine the set of circumstances in more detail, we can see that the initial trauma for her parents was having a child with a disability. This led them to become quite obsessive about trying to get the best for her to compensate for her disability. This was the beginning of treating Miranda as a problem instead of as a child, and this in itself was traumatising for Miranda. Her parents and their continued search for a solution – for a service which was not available, for the right educational placement that may be able to provide what they couldn't, to make her better – was unhelpful. Being sent away to a residential placement was traumatising for Miranda and this came on top of her primary trauma, so compounded her difficulties and led to the development of maladaptive behaviours.

While attending the residential school, Miranda was subjected to at least one sexual assault, although the details could never be proven. This was a further trauma for her and for her parents who became obsessed with looking for the perpetrator. We can see how this is building up to be a situation of multiple traumas without resolution. And at the base of this is a young woman with an emotional developmental age of 12 to 18 months, unable to process her experiences. The raw emotion that she expressed became too much for her parents to cope with, and their response was to become obsessed with filling her life with activities and distractions so as not to think about the bad things that had happened.

Sadly, in a situation like this, there are limited possibilities for progress. There is no obvious therapeutic support for the parents, because they don't meet any criteria for needing mental health services or therapy. Secondly, there is limited understanding from commissioners and service providers of the needs of an adult woman who is emotionally still an infant. Fortunately, most of the time, Miranda was able to be provided with staff who could tolerate her demanding behaviour, recognise to some extent what was causing it, and provide her with an acceptable level of support. Sadly, however, this could only maintain her at her present level; it could not facilitate development to the next level. The possibilities of her reaching individuation, a sense of self as a separate independent being, were very limited with the level of support being offered.

This is a very complex situation for people to find themselves in, although not uncommon. Processing trauma is always difficult, and processing early trauma is even more so because it is more difficult to accept. It is extremely painful for parents to reflect on their impact on the child as well as the impact of the child on them. As a society, we don't provide the level and type of support that is needed. We are perhaps better in the 21st century than we were in the 20th, but we still have a long way to go. If we can get to a position where every life is valued then people with complex disabilities and trauma will have a better chance of getting their needs met and leading a more fulfilled life.

The research into the impact of trauma does show that people can move on in terms of their emotional self at any age, provided they have what they need. The four components of trauma informed care don't change. The first, and most important, is the availability of a reliable significant other at all times. This doesn't have to be the same person, but there must be a formal handover from one person to the next. The individual must know at all times who that significant person is if their anxiety is to remain under control. The second component is enough staff to make sure the environment is safe. The third component is that those staff should be trained and supported to provide the emotional support that the individual needs. The fourth component is individual therapy to address the initial trauma and subsequent trauma.

If these four components are provided, then emotional development will happen. Miranda is still waiting for them to be provided.

Chapter 15: George

What happens when traumatised people escalate to secure settings?

We come now to a very sad story of a young man from a very troubled background who ended up in a secure setting. At the time that I first met him, George was being regularly held by several staff, who would sit on him to control him, and he would spend a lot of time fighting them.

Since then, I have met several young men in similar situations, and as they could perhaps be identified, I'm going to mix up their stories to some extent, adding and subtracting facts that do not detract from the main theme. George was about 35 at the time of my first intervention with him. He had a chequered history of detentions in prison and hospitals. He had a diagnosis of an intellectual disability, which had led to him being diverted from prison into the secure hospital system. The offences for which he was detained included violence against people causing grievous bodily harm. There was no doubt that he could be very frightening. There was also evidence of him having injured people in the past. But one of the unexpected consequences of his behaviour, and the approach to looking after him, was that many staff were securing lots of overtime hours and consequent payments. This had an impact on their willingness to do something different, on the basis of understanding his behaviour better, as opposed to just stopping him from hurting others.

The study of his behaviour showed that he was not completely isolated, and did gain some satisfaction from interacting with other people. An observation of his behaviour put him clearly into the early rapprochement stage of emotional development, equivalent to that of a two-year-old. It was very difficult to get support staff to accept that his behaviour was not driven by intent to harm them, but by a maladaptive way of trying to communicate.

When we look again at the trauma informed care model, we can see that George was in a placement that was not threatened by his behaviour so could be seen to be a safe place. It is always difficult to get people to understand that a safe place is different from a secure place, although it can look the same. A safe place includes an emotionally nurturing environment, and this is not readily available in secure settings, where the attempt is always to try and make the individual behave appropriately, usually by using some form of behavioural incentive, or the withdrawal of attention and other punitive approaches, including seclusion with no contact.

The next requirement for good trauma informed care is sufficient staff to make the world safe and maintain the emotional environment at the correct level. There was no doubt that George had sufficient staff but there were questions to be asked about their role. They clearly saw their role as controlling George and minimising injury to him and themselves. What I needed them to do was to engage with George with appropriate activities for his cognitive age, but in a way that was appropriate for his emotional developmental stage. If it was possible to do that, then there would be an expectation that he would be able to manage with less staff, learn more, and choose to behave in a more socially acceptable way. To do that, the staff would need to engage in the third requirement of good trauma informed care.

The third requirement is that the staff are trained and supported to provide an emotionally nurturing environment. This required that all staff looking after George, and people like George, should at a minimum engage in learning that all behaviour has meaning. This training looks at a specific behaviour or range of behaviours from a behavioural, cognitive, psychodynamic, and systems perspective. If we analyse a particular behaviour from those four perspectives, it is very easy to see which one makes the most sense, and which would be the most likely to be effective in helping George to change. When we looked at George in the environment in which he found himself, we could see that the behavioural approach was clearly not working, and was unlikely to work as he had no relationship with the people trying to teach him. We only learn to behave differently when we care about what the people teaching us think of us. And to do that we have to have reached the emotional developmental stage of at least late rapprochement, and preferably individuation. As a consequence, the behavioural approach was going to have no impact.

The cognitive approach also requires that there is a good relationship with the person needing the intervention. It also requires that the person whose behaviour we want to change can think through the impact of their behaviour on other people. This requires a reasonable level of intellect, as well as the developmental stage of late rapprochement or individuation. So, again, the cognitive approach was unlikely to be effective with George.

When we look at psychodynamic approaches, we are considering the emotional world of the individual, and particularly early development. This includes, and is probably highly significant, the primary relationship with the primary carer, usually the mother. When we looked into George's history, it was clear that his relationship with his mother had never been good and that he had had a very chaotic start to his life. The fact that he was functioning at an emotional developmental stage of early rapprochement confirmed this. As a consequence, it was indicated that an essential part of an intervention with George would have to include the development of a secure emotional relationship. Psychodynamic psychotherapy was indicated along with the staff being trained to provide an emotionally nurturing environment to support therapy.

This thinking led to considering a systems approach. Systems approaches are very often needed but rarely made to work because of the complexity of the human mind, and of social systems. If we consider what's been said above about what is needed, then clearly there is a system, a systematic approach, that needs to be in place to facilitate all the aspects of the therapeutic intervention.

Whenever we consider a system, we have to look at what goes in and what comes out. There are simple electrical and water systems that most of us can understand. However, human relationship systems are more complex. The simplest human relation system is the family, where you have, hopefully, an adult parental group, and a child group, with clear lines and expectations of behaviour from each. A family group where parents are confident, competent and reliable will generally produce children who are confident and develop well, reaching individuation with a secure sense of who they are and where they fit in the world. The systems approach in a secure unit set-up is possible if all of the components are in place. It requires detailed clarity about roles and responsibilities, and absolute reliability on essentials like food, clothing and personal care so that there is no fear of being hungry or dirty. The next component is, of course, the reliability of people and staff, to be in the parental role of being reliable, confirming, and facilitating development. It is essential that they are not overcontrolling, negative, emotionally absent or cruel. Maintaining the positive attributes of the parental role is essential. And it must be remembered that a 35-year-old man who has been traumatised in early childhood is going to be very suspicious of staff who change their behaviour towards him. This is one of the main reasons why the staff must be supported in their role so that they can process the feelings that they experience in response to projections from George.

The fourth component is individual therapy, and the information described above would indicate that psychodynamic therapy is what was required. Somebody so distressed and traumatised would require short therapy sessions of 20 to 30 minutes, twice a week, building up to longer sessions over time. Initially, it may be necessary for someone like George to have staff with him in his therapy sessions. This would only need to last until he developed a trusting relationship with this therapist, at which time he would be able to manage 1:1 sessions. In a situation like this, there are elements to consider about the safety of the therapist as well as the safety of George.

It has been possible to put this model in place occasionally, although it is not easy to secure the acceptance of all the professionals involved. People like George are often detained under the Mental Health Act and this can either help or hinder, depending on the understanding from others about the need for the therapeutic approach. Understandably, staff will be wary, especially if they know people who have been injured in the past. But if nothing is done to help George grow emotionally, the destructive and aggressive behaviour is likely to continue for many more years.

It has been my experience that it is possible to put this in place and facilitate real change. However, the early damage from trauma can be so severe that full recovery is unlikely to be possible. It is a real positive if there is some recovery. If we consider that George was functioning at the two-year-old stage of emotional development, then we can reflect on the fact that two-year-olds can be quite pleasant and quite good fun for quite a lot of the time so long as they are not tired, or over-challenged, or made to feel overlooked and uncared for. It follows that enabling George to find the positive aspects of his emotional developmental stage would significantly improve his quality of life. He may never get to the stage where he can move on to late rapprochement and individuation. He may never get to a point where he can leave a secure setting. But if he can live in that setting without having several staff with him at all times, and without causing injuries to himself or others, then there would be signs of maturity and positive aspects to his life and for those around him.

It has distressed me throughout my career to find people like George living in such oppressive circumstances for years on end. I have argued, and will continue to argue, that using this emotional development therapeutic approach makes a huge difference.

Chapter 16: Margaret

It's never too late to put in place a therapeutic approach and make a difference.

I first met Margaret when she was in her early 40s and living in a residential facility for people with intellectual disabilities and additional needs. She had nursing staff to look after her so it must have been a registered nursing home. The owner of the facility had asked me if I would go and see her as the staff were struggling to meet her needs. She was having significant outbursts of screaming and lashing out, requiring restraint to be used. This was, of course, upsetting for everyone – staff and other residents. The owner was close to thinking that Margaret would have to move back to a hospital setting but was hoping that this might be avoided.

Margaret and I made an instant connection which was helpful. I had an opportunity to look through her records and knew that she had a mild intellectual disability, a diagnosis of borderline personality disorder, now referred to as emotionally unstable personality disorder, and that she had been in many care facilities, including hospitals. She had moved to her present placement from a secure hospital.

Margaret could talk fluently so was able to tell me about some of her experiences. We agreed to meet weekly for therapeutic sessions and this continued for several years, fortunately funded within the agreed contract that I had with the home. What became very clear was that Margaret had a very disturbed early life and was hospitalised in her early teens as her family were not able to cope with her sudden changes of mood and behaviour. She was able to talk about her family, and her life experiences that had been difficult. We were able to look at traumatic life events, explore the impact and meaning of them, and reach some level of resolution. She did very well in therapy, was able to maintain her placement, eventually moving on to supportive living in the community.

When we look at the impact of early trauma on Margaret, we find that this related primarily to abuse from her brothers in the family setting. This had disturbed the development of a sense of herself as a good-enough person. In the emotional developmental model, she was stuck between practicing and early rapprochement, with lots of repetitive behaviours and an inability to maintain relationships with other people. It follows that an essential part of her care must include the availability of a significant other at all times. In a busy residential care facility, this is not easy to establish or maintain. However, we were able to identify six members of staff who, between them, could make sure that at least one of them was on duty across the days and weeks, enabling us to put in place a rota of significant others for Margaret. Once that was in place and Margaret knew who to go to if she was struggling with her thoughts or feelings, there was an immediate reduction in her anxiety. Once the anxiety in Margaret was reduced, there was a consequent reduction in anxiety in the staff. This had a cumulative effect across the whole establishment, and all benefited from the calmer atmosphere.

Once that emotional support was in place, it became possible to look at ways that Margaret could continue her emotional development to a more mature stage. Over the next two or three years she became much more stable, able to engage with people, able to go out and about and on holiday. Some of the more distressing behaviours that had been there, including self-harm, reduced dramatically and her quality of life consequently improved.

As Margaret was cognitively more able than most of the people I've talked about, there was a higher expectation from staff that she would be able to choose to behave in a better way. That is, better for herself as well as for the environment and for other people. But emotionally she was not at the level of being able to negotiate, which comes with late rapprochement, so was constantly falling short of expectations and suffering anxiety through not being understood. On reflection, it does seem to me that people of average intelligence with a diagnosis of emotionally unstable 'personality disorder' may all benefit from a similar approach. This would fit with my experience of working in community settings with people with this diagnosis. It may be that the condition is in fact a condition of arrested emotional development and could be treated in a similar way. In my experience, it is usually treated with medication, and it may be that this works because the recipient trusts the prescriber – another factor on top of the calming effect of the medication which may be highly significant.

As time went on and Margaret became more amenable to collective activities, she was able to go on holidays, out shopping, and take part in activities like garden parties that were open to the public. She began to show skill in craftwork and to make items that were suitable for presents or for sale. This gave her enormous satisfaction and pleasure.

Another factor that came into play was her interest in her family of origin. As much of the negative experience that had led to her condition was within the family, it was quite a strained set of relationships. However, as her understanding increased, she became able to relate to some of her family. Her parents were no longer alive, so it was with her brothers and sisters that she made contact. She was even able to forgive the brothers who had abused her. One of these relationships became significant, supportive and more equal, giving her a sense of belonging and immense pleasure.

As Margaret was able to speak and recount stories of her life, it was possible to chart the incidents that had led to her presentation at the time of our meeting. There was a long story of failed placements, including hospitals, hostels, marriages, and other care homes. Analysis of the breakdowns of the placements indicated that the issue was always the same. A breakdown in trusting relationships was the key factor, and it was clear that the individuals concerned were not aware of how important they had become to Margaret. As a consequence, it was usually Margaret who was blamed when things went wrong. Most of the time she was eager to please in her seeking of positive regard from people. She could never understand why people did not value her, a feature of the early emotional developmental stage at which she was stuck.

When I look back on the intervention that was put in place and the success that followed, I am struck by the fact that Margaret had so many years of misery before finding a therapeutic environment that could help her. It is comforting to know that she did in time get what she needed with a single-person service of supported living in the community. One of the positives about single-person services is that there is always a significant other present and this is key to the provision of an emotionally nurturing environment. Some people will reach a point of individuation and be able to manage without the staff support. I suspect this varies according to the severity and complexity of the initial trauma, and the age at which it is possible to put in place the right intervention. Margaret was already a mature lady. She had had many relationships which had failed and caused further damage to her self-esteem and identity. So, she still needed staff with her but could live in harmony with them, with no outbursts or self-harm, and a decent quality of life. She was able to engage in the community and make craftwork presents for others from which she got positive feedback.

Hopefully, the service provider for Margaret will recognise what works and be willing to provide that for other similar people. There does seem to be some resistance to 24-hour single-person services as they are quite expensive. But they are nothing like as expensive as hospital treatment or regular trips to accident and emergency following self-harming and the other consequences of not providing what people need. We would always hope that the difficulties are identified in childhood, and sufficient support is put in place to facilitate their emotional development, but if it isn't then the individuals must be provided with what they need to cope with the world.

The impact of trauma on Margaret was significant. Her early life experiences led to institutional responses from quite a young age. This compounded the trauma with a lack of understanding, an absence of emotionally nurturing support, further punishment when her behaviour led to restraint and seclusion, and the general absence of positive regard and love. I bring her here into this text as an example of someone who is cognitively more able, although still with a mild intellectual disability, where her emotional disability has been her major difficulty, and it has not been recognised at an early stage. I hope that we will come to a better understanding of emotional disability for people in the future.

Chapter 17: Lillian

This chapter looks at the usefulness of the emotional developmental stage model with older people becoming incapacitated by dementia.

I'm going to move on now to the application of the theoretical model to all the people in the process of loss of ability through dementia. Having followed the slow deterioration that Lillian went through from the first onset to when she passed away, I became aware of the relevant interactive styles and behaviours that were happening in reverse to what I was finding with the people with intellectual and emotional disabilities.

There was a clear history in Lillian's life of early trauma, and some repeated trauma throughout her life. There then followed, in her early 80s, a series of transient ischaemic attacks that involved falls and broken bones. This inevitably led to hospital visits, some hospitalisations, some surgery, and long periods of recuperation. What became obvious to us over time was that her ability to relate to the people she knew and the medical staff changed. She had worked as a health professional all her life and was a competent and intelligent person, with good personal interactive skills – fully individuated in terms of her emotional development.

After the onset of the TIAs, she began to seek assistance, to lose confidence in her decision-making ability and was clearly functioning at the level of the late rapprochement stage. She became less able to make decisions for herself but was able to join in with some straightforward problem-solving like what to have for tea, what to wear, and ordinary day-to-day decision-making.

After about another six to 12 months, and further falls, Lillian became progressively more dependent on others to make decisions for her. However, she was still happy to engage with people and enjoyed going out and about on visits to ice cream parlours and such. This was very much in tune with the early rapprochement stage, where two-way interaction was comfortable, but the ability to make decisions for herself was limited.

Lillian slowly declined into the practicing stage, spending most of her time engaged in repetitive behaviours, and reduced the amount of interaction that she was comfortable with or that she could tolerate with other people.

So long as her need to know that there was somebody there to keep the world safe was met, she was reasonably content, but she could become distressed if she couldn't see who was there for her. She developed some security behaviours like holding onto soft toys. She also developed the equivalent of the red 'wellies' situation that we find in young children, when she had specific clothes that she wanted to wear every time. If this is recognised by all the people for what it is, in other words, the need for security, then it can be accepted and not challenged. This makes life more tolerable for the person going through the stages of dementia.

Inevitably, her deterioration continued until Lillian was not interacting with people, and was maintaining her basic sense of security with her chair, and in bed – the equivalent of the pram or the cot. This is the differentiation stage of emotional development, only reached in reverse through dementia-related decline. If this emotional regression is recognised, acknowledged and accommodated, there is a marked reduction in anxiety in the person with dementia. That core ingredient – the availability of a significant other security figure – is essential for people going through dementia in the same way that it is essential for little children going through the stages in the development of self.

That loss of self in dementia is extremely painful for families, partners and care staff to witness. However, having a model for understanding what is happening emotionally, with the loss of self, can empower people to maintain the quality of life for as long as possible. Anything that reduces anxiety must be good. Not all people with dementia go through the same stages in the same way, or at least not with the same anxiety, and this may link to whatever trauma they may have experienced before the onset of dementia. I have certainly known people who have shown all the same signs of the progressive loss of self, but have not been distressed by it. It would require an extensive piece of research on some very detailed histories to work out the role of trauma in this process. But knowing what we know of the impact of trauma on development from birth to self, it is likely that there is a similar process impacting the ability to adjust to the dementia process.

It is extremely distressing to see people with dementia and anxiety. They often look extremely frightened and may lash out in fear. Having a model of understanding the emotional process must be helpful to those supporting individuals with dementia. As already mentioned, trauma memories likely play a big part, but it is as yet unproven. The thinking is included here in this book as it is relevant.

Inevitably the end result is death. Although a person with advanced dementia who has reached the differentiation stage may appear to not be relating to other people, it is likely that they are still aware of the emotional presence of another person so it is important that somebody sits with them as they fade away, if they are awake. Hopefully, most people will die quietly in their sleep and, if their anxiety has been contained by the provision of a safe emotional environment, that is more likely to be what happens. And perhaps that is what most of us can hope for.

Lillian's story can be replicated in most care homes and families living at home. The early rapprochement stage can be very trying, where the repetitive demands can be met but then continue to happen. I visit one care home regularly and there is one lady there who constantly asks for the toilet. She is clearly showing anxiety about having an accident, and this may be linked to traumatic incidents from childhood, but it is very trying for staff who feel that they are letting her down if they don't take her, but know she doesn't really need to go. She still trusts that she will get a response, demonstrating that she is in the stage of early rapprochement, with high anxiety as she can no longer take herself, but still aware of the bodily function. That control gets progressively lost and the use of inco pads becomes normal. This, too, can be distressing or comforting, depending on the links to early life experiences.

It would be useful for all support and care staff to know about emotional disability and the stage model that is the basis of the FAIT. It gives confidence to them if they understand what is behind lots of anxiety behaviours.

Chapter 18: Richard

Catastrophic breakdowns can still respond to a therapeutic approach that goes further than looking after physical needs.

Richard is somebody I've known for many years. When I first met him, he was working full-time in a competent senior position, living alone after a divorce, but quite content with life. Over time, he met someone else, married again, and moved to a new house with his new wife. He continued to work and contribute to the local community through activities as a charity trustee and such like. He was clearly fully individuated, enjoying a good quality of life and happy with his position in the world.

Richard is like most of us, going through life and its various stages with limited hiccups. He did, again like most of us, have some traumatic events that had impacted on him. It was never clear what they might have been in his early life, but he was clearly traumatised by the breakup of his first marriage. He had some difficult relationships with his adult children, and these caused him some distress. Outwardly, though, he showed no signs of any serious psychological difficulties.

Then things began to change. In his late 70s, he started to become forgetful, became argumentative, and was less pleasant to be with. If we look at this from the perspective of the emotional developmental stage model, we can recognise the slow loss of his individuality and competence. He began to need lots of reassurance, lots of help with decision-making, and lots of patience when he became frustrated and lost his temper. It became difficult to have discussions with him in charity meetings. It became very difficult for his wife to cope with ordinary day-to-day decision-making as he became more argumentative.

In the next stage of his deterioration into the early rapprochement stage, he became quite obsessed with the television, needing to have it on all the time. He also suffered from loss of hearing and so the television had to be quite loud. This was quite oppressive for his wife and any visitors to the house. At this stage, he was still engaging in discussions about choices over food and activities or TV programmes. He was also still able to manage his personal care, like toileting and shaving. He was quite argumentative and needed a lot of attention. He could become quite sulky if he felt he was being ignored, in the same way that we find this with very young children.

As he moved into the practicing stage, he developed more repetitive behaviours. There was more rigidity about where he would sit and where others would sit in the room. He would spend long periods looking through the same magazine over and over. He became less attentive to his appearance, and it was difficult to persuade him to shave and have his hair cut. He was still talking, and still able to engage in conversation to some extent, although this became increasingly repetitive. Talking about things that were important to him when he was younger generally worked quite well. It was very sad for those of us who knew him to see him disappear in this way. However, it was helpful to have the emotional developmental model to help us to understand what was happening in response to his dementia.

After some months of being quite stuck in the practicing stage, Richard had a major breakdown and suddenly became unable to walk. It was difficult to know if this had been a stroke, some other brain incident, or a psychological response to the fear of recognising his condition. This is something we will never know, but what we do know is that he became bedbound and very clearly in the differentiation stage of emotional development. His world was his bed, and everything that happened, happened there. His food was brought to him, and he needed help to eat it, having lost the coordination of hand to mouth. All his physical needs had to be attended to. However, he remained cheerful and attempted to talk to people, usually with a big smile, but also with partial sentences, as he was unable to complete a full thought. It was of course distressing to see someone who had been so competent slip into an infantile state.

We knew very little about Richard's early life so we don't know much about what may have been traumatic for him as a youngster. What we can see is the trauma he experienced in the early stages of the onset of dementia, when he was aware of what was happening. His behaviour in the early stages was difficult as he became more argumentative and sometimes aggressive.

It is only recently that I have begun to see the usefulness of the model of understanding emotional development in reverse in dementia. I have only included two examples in this book, but I want to make it clear that it is a useful model in helping the person with dementia to have a decent quality of life if their emotional needs are met in the right way at the right stages. The need for the security of a significant other is crucial, particularly in the rapprochement and practicing stages. By the time they reach the differentiation stage, they are usually dependent on the physical environment for that sense of security. So long as the bed or chair doesn't change, and the immediate surroundings don't change, most people can be quite relaxed, with manageable anxiety.

We can speculate on what happened to Richard and what tipped him into that immobile situation. The brain scans did not show anything that could explain what had happened. It can only be speculation, as it cannot be proven, that it was so traumatic for him to recognise his loss of ability that he psychologically shut down and became unable to function. He certainly seemed more content once he had 'given up' and could accept being treated as a dependent person. We will never know, but it may be that he had struggled most of his life to be independent. There may have been traumatic events in his past relationships that had left him feeling in need of care and attention. Once he was bedbound, he had to be looked after, and it may be that this is what he always needed but could only have it when he reached the stage of advanced dementia.

I hope that there will be more recognition of the emotional world of people who are losing their sense of self through the dementia process. I don't think it matters what sort of dementia or other brain deterioration is involved. So long as the emotional environment provides safety in human relationships, people do seem to be able to have manageable anxiety and to cope with what is happening to them. It does seem, also, that families may benefit from having an understanding of their role and what treatment helps as their loved one deteriorates. They may not feel so helpless, which can only be good at very difficult times.

Chapter 19: Rose

Can we help people whose cognitive skills lead to assumptions of competence?

So far, we've concentrated mainly on people with some level of cognitive disability, either through a long-standing condition of intellectual disability or through the more recently acquired disability through dementia. What we've been trying to look at is the impact of trauma on people who have already got some difficulties. I want now to go on to think about Rose, a young woman of high intellectual ability ready to go off to university, but with a diagnosis of high-functioning autism, previously known as Asperger's, and the relevance to her of ideas of emotional disability.

Rose had some inpatient treatment as a teenager because of her mental health struggles. Much of this was related to the difficulty of her diagnosis of autism. This was rejected by her parents, and to a large extent by herself. She knew she was extremely uncomfortable in her own skin and developed an eating disorder in response. This led to the hospitalisation and to some long-term therapy for her after discharge. It was clear from her presentation that, in emotional developmental terms, she was functioning at the stage of differentiation. All of her behaviours were self-referenced, she struggled to look outside of herself and her own distress, and it became clear that she had spent much of her life observing others. Despite this emotional difficulty, she had attended well to her learning and was succeeding educationally. This ability seemed to be masking her difficulties, and both her school and family were unable to see how much she was suffering.

After her discharge from hospital, there were concerns about how she could be supported in the community and at college. Individual twice-weekly therapy was organised for her, with the clear plan of encouraging her to learn to look after herself and to develop an ability to relate to others. The therapy needed to be based on attachment needs, rather than a cognitive behavioural approach. She was exceptionally bright and could see through any of the superficial technique-based therapies. Fortunately, she engaged well with the therapeutic process, although there were times when she became so distressed that she was at risk of self-harm. She was given a helpline and used this from time to time when she felt at risk of taking her own life.

Over a period of three years, Rose moved through the emotional developmental stages to individuation and was able to go off to university with a clearer understanding of herself and where she fits in the world. Throughout the period of therapy, she became attached to her therapist and could recognise them as her significant other. She was given telephone and text access outside of the therapy sessions and this was crucial to her recovery. The family relationships had deteriorated and this phenomenon had to be processed during the therapy. She was eventually able to recognise the traumatic events of her early childhood and the impact these had had on her later development. Some of the difficulties were about gender values within the family. Some of them were about a lack of understanding of her superior intellect. Collectively, they amounted to an experience of not being seen or valued as herself throughout her childhood. This left her, as a teenager, feeling very lost and engaging in behaviours such as not eating and self-harming that could be interpreted as a cry for help. The hospitalisation had probably saved her from starving to death but had not been able to address the root cause of her distress. She was fortunate in being given the long-term therapy as an outpatient. This would possibly not have been funded if she was not at risk of further inpatient treatment. This is one of the difficulties with the criteria for long-term funding for therapy. One of the arguments for the recognition of emotional disability as a condition is to help with the applications for long-term interventions. Many of the people who need this sort of intervention are the ones who may go on to need long-term inpatient treatment or residential care, which is much more expensive. Sadly, many therapists nowadays are not trained to provide long-term, attachment-based therapy.

Flexibility of approach was also a key component. The lack of family support meant that the therapist had to go to Rose or the sessions wouldn't happen. This commitment from the therapist was novel for Rose and had a positive impact on her self-esteem. It became clear over time that her family did care but were unfamiliar with therapy interventions and struggled to see the value of short sessions every week. It is not uncommon for people, including professionals, to fail to see the value of the 'secure base' of regular therapy that John Bowlby describes in *A secure base: Parent-child attachment and healthy human development* (1988). In the model being used in this book, it is the 'significant other' that is provided. Ideally, all children have this throughout the formative three to four years from birth. Fortunately, most children do get this but sadly there is not enough understanding in mainstream services to help those where there are difficulties. There will usually be recognised difficulties with difficult births and early identification of disability, but anyone can have difficulty establishing their relationship with their newborn or small child. It seems imperative that neonatal staff, including midwives, health visitors and paediatricians should have access to more knowledge about emotional development and the impact of early trauma.

I will go on to discuss in more detail, in a later chapter, the issues around therapy and the trauma informed model of support and understanding.

There were some difficult times during the three years of therapy for Rose. There were a number of suicide threats, some cutting, continued issues around food, and rejection by family. However, she gradually managed to process what had happened to her in her early childhood, to address and tolerate strained relationships with her peer group at college, and to learn to value herself. It was a joy to see her blossom and complete her studies ready for university. Her superior intellect was an issue for her college staff and she learned to blend in better so as not to challenge. In time, she developed a concern for her fellow students and was supportive of those struggling with depression. She came to accept that she was on a different life path from the one expected from her birth origins, as she embraced this path as her own.

Chapter 20: Susan

We look now at someone stuck for many years before receiving the right approach to her trauma.

I first met Susan in her mid-30s when I was asked to assess her suitability for supportive living. At the time, she was living in a residential care facility for people with intellectual disabilities and was clearly not happy. She had some verbal ability, and expectations of her were quite high as she was considered to be more able than many of her housemates. What was being missed was the de-synchrony between her cognitive ability and her emotional ability. The assessment with the Frankish Assessment for the Impact of Trauma showed that many of her behaviours fell into the differentiation stage and the practicing stage, indicating that her emotional age was approximately one year. Clearly, this was very different from her cognitive age and her physical age. It was understandable that her support staff, who had no extra specific training in emotional disability, were finding her frustrating to support. There were constant clashes as expectations of her were too high, and her response was infantile behaviour that was frowned upon.

Susan had a particular attachment to her dolls and had quite a collection. However, it was considered by her support staff to be inappropriate for her to play with dolls in her 30s and they were therefore confined to her room. If she wanted to be with the dolls, she had to be in her room. Another aspect of the dolls that was very disturbing was that she would pull off their heads or arms and legs. Staff and other clients found this very distressing, and, at this stage, it was not understood. However, if we reflect on her emotional stage and the clash with the expectations placed upon her, it's possible to see the significance of the attacks on the dolls. They could be seen as a projection of her anger towards herself and her inability to please people, or to have her needs met. They could also be seen as unresolved anger which is evident in people who have not reached the emotional developmental stage of being able to tolerate good and bad aspects in the same person. Melanie Klein speaks about this in some detail in *Envy and Gratitude* (1955) and refers to the resolution of the depressive position as that point at which understanding and tolerance of both good and bad in a significant other can be reached. In neurotypical development, where all is going well, the day the child recognises that the mother cannot meet all of their needs instantly and can accept this, is a momentous day and the point at which the resolution is reached. There is a period before full acceptance of good and bad in the same person which is a demanding time for support staff if it hasn't happened in the ordinary course of development. And, of course, it is different if the person is in a care situation.

To help Susan, she was provided with her room and her dolls. She was allowed to have as many dolls as she needed, initially. She was provided with the emotional support of a named significant other at all times. She would often choose to stay in her room so couldn't see her significant other, but she quickly learned that the person was present whenever needed. She was also able to take her dolls out of the room, usually one at a time, and was encouraged to relate to the dolls in a positive way, caring for them and keeping them safe. This was replicating what was being provided for her and it didn't take too long for her to respond to this positive approach. She gradually became able to relate to more people, to spend more time out of her room, and to access her cognitive ability more frequently and more positively.

Over time, the differentiation behaviours reduced. These were self-referenced behaviours, where she withdrew from contact with others and cocooned herself in her room, in her bed with her dolls. There was an increase in practicing behaviours, which were repetitive and could be seen as a bit irritating by some people, but they were part of her necessary developmental process and progress. Play with the dolls would follow a set pattern for several weeks and then another behaviour would come into play. For example, Susan would carry a doll around with her as if it were a baby, engaging other people in conversation about the baby doll, and all would respond appropriately. Over time, with the development of early rapprochement behaviours, she started to engage with people about other things as well as the doll. It became clear that Susan was recognising the value of a relationship with other people, human people, and her need for a safe relationship with her dolls reduced. She became able to go out without a doll, and she stopped destroying them. It is important to recognise that this behaviour had been present for over 20 years and only changed when her emotional needs were met.

Because of the extreme delay in emotional development, it was suspected that there had been major familial trauma very early in her life. There was very little information available as she had been in one care situation after another since being a small child. It was therefore decided that the fourth element of trauma informed care, individual psychotherapy, was required as well as providing an emotionally nurturing environment. Susan continues to receive some therapy. She has never been able to progress to working for more than ten to 15 minutes at a time. Her ability to trust people is severely impaired, but her attachment and security to the environment have strengthened to the point where she feels safe, nurtured, not judged, and is able to function to the best of her ability.

One of the very notable things that occurred after some years of intervention is that she started to make choices and to trust that her choices would be met. She began to express her opinion in group situations and to ask for things that she wanted. These are all evidence of progression into early rapprochement, to the recognition of the value of relationships, and the ability to bond in two-way situations. It is again important to stress that none of this had happened in previous placements and only became possible and successful when she was provided with what she needed emotionally, and there was enough patience to allow her to develop at her own pace. As has been mentioned in some previous chapters, the time it took for her to move from differentiation to early rapprochement was approximately the same time as it would take in neurotypical development. Once achieved, the evidence would suggest that it is not lost and the ability to function at the higher level is maintained over time. Clearly, it would not be appropriate to test this out by offering a different type of support. Theoretically, it would only be expected to be permanently maintained if the individual reaches individuation. There is an argument for maintaining the support at the appropriate level as the quality of life is significantly improved. The further people can move along the emotional developmental progression the better. Anyone who can engage in two-way interaction in a meaningful way will have a better quality of life than those who can't.

Chapter 21: Florence

Here we explore the case of another young woman who has been misunderstood for many years after suffering extensive trauma in her early life.

Florence first came to my attention when she was in her early 40s, having had a very stressful life up to that point, including significant familial abuse and multiple attempts to keep her safe and provide her with an appropriate support package. She was frequently referred to as 'hard work', mainly because of her constant talking and asking questions. Rather than see these as irritating, in the emotional developmental model they were seen as representative of her insecurity and fear. She was constantly checking that the world, or the people around her, was stable, secure and reliable. She found it extremely difficult to believe that she was going to receive what she needed in terms of support. One way of looking at the behaviour could be seen as attention seeking, and this was how it had been treated in the past. This phenomenon is usually seen in a negative light. However, if we look at it in an emotional deprivation light, we can see that it arises because the need for attention was not met in childhood, and has led to emotional developmental delay.

Assessment showed the behaviour to be solidly in the practicing stage, repetitive, and engaged in because that was what she could do. She could talk, so she did. And she talked and talked and talked. At times this was extremely stressful for other people, but once it was understood, it became easier for people to respond. Once people did respond and, in addition, engage directly with Florence, rather than waiting for her to initiate contact, the tension was significantly reduced and relationships improved. This led quite quickly to strong development into the early rapprochement stage of the emotional developmental model.

Florence was able to engage with other people, leading to initiating conversation, rather than talking at someone, and this became more rewarding for everyone. Over time, it became evident that Florence was developing problem-solving skills and moving into late rapprochement, where she could negotiate and accept the results of negotiation without resorting to over-talking. This happened over a period of a couple of years and has led to developments, including being able to choose where she wants to live and what sort of life she wants to lead. This must be seen as a positive outcome for anyone with an intellectual disability, an abuse history, and years of being criticised for behaviour that results from emotional deprivation.

It is worth speculating on why so many service providers and professionals find so-called attention-seeking behaviour a problem. It is always described negatively in meetings and reports. If a behavioural approach is used then the person is ignored when engaging in attention-seeking behaviour, and this, of course, is the complete opposite of what is needed. It consequently increases the behaviour, rather than decreasing it. And, inevitably, the individual engaging in the behaviour is the one who gets blamed. I have puzzled over why this particular behaviour is such a problem and have come to the realisation that it stems from the emotional pain that is projected from somebody who is emotionally developmentally delayed. The projections, which most professionals with disability clients will not have much knowledge of, can be difficult to understand and tolerate. Staff training in trauma informed care must involve awareness of and response to projections. This is another psychoanalytic element that is rejected by a strong behavioural model but can be absorbed and used in the trauma informed care model. The correct behavioural intervention and support can be provided using the ideas that run through this book, and it is important to recognise that an approach which is based on deep psychoanalytic thinking can be provided on a day-to-day basis by support staff so long as they are trained in the basics of what they are meant to be doing. Individual psychotherapy, with a strong relationship between the client and the therapist, may be crucial to recovery. In the trauma informed care model, the relationship between the staff, the support staff support, and the recipient of services is crucial.

Florence's quality of life has improved, such that she is now able to offer support to other people with an element of understanding of how important people are to each other. It has allowed her to develop her self-esteem and consequently a sense of being useful. This is a significant progression from where she was when I first met her.

The House Tree Person (HTP) assessment was used with Florence. The pictures she drew initially indicated insecurity, arrested ego development, and identity problems. A retest at a later date showed more security, more clarity of ego development, and a more positive identity. The HTP is a very powerful test and must be used carefully. When it was first developed it was used in therapy with children. I have adapted it to be used as an assessment tool for people with disabilities (see chapter 4). It was very valuable in evaluating the impact of trauma informed care for Florence.

There are many people like Florence who have been misunderstood for many years, often treated as a problem because of their erratic behaviour, without any understanding of the meaning of the behaviour. It would seem likely that Florence's constant talking came from feelings of not being seen and heard when she was little, but then persisting as she was re-traumatised by the people who were irritated by her talking. What needs to happen now, and fortunately does most of the time, is that people give her good eye contact and engage her in conversation. This usually leads to an appropriate and short interaction, relaxation and reduction in anxiety, and then moving on to other activities. If we reflect on this in a young child of less than two years old, we know how important it is to nurture development with positive interaction. What we also know is that many children do not receive that level of positive regard during the critical developmental phases of their life. Before beginning this work looking at emotional development, I, like many others, thought that the repetitive behaviours could be a fixed state and not amenable to alteration. This was of course the model of the old hospital care, where people with persistent behaviours were detained and provided with usually good physical care, but with little understanding of their emotional needs. What the work in this book describes is a way forward from that, with significant evidence for the fact that people can make progress with their emotional development if their basic emotional needs are met. We must understand that someone who is emotionally less than three years old will be traumatised by lots of ordinary experiences because of expectations that they can respond in an age-appropriate way. If they were able to respond in an age-appropriate way, and behave in socially acceptable ways, they would not generally be referred to services but would live happily at home with an ordinary life. Many families do want to support their intellectually disabled offspring and many persevere for a very long time. With a better understanding of the meaning of behaviour, they have an opportunity to keep the family together longer, if that is their wish. Their offspring also have more opportunities to leave the family home and have an ordinary life as adults if they reach a stage at which they can be mature enough to engage with regular services. It does seem like a very simple idea, and it is difficult to understand why it has taken so long for it to be more readily accepted. It is very positive for me, after working with this model for approximately 40 years, to realise that more people are open to the ideas of emotional development and emotional disability. It has certainly made a significant difference to Florence's life.

Chapter 22: The experience of locked units

Here, we consider the extreme end of provision for those whose trauma is missed, leading to an escalation to secure provision.

During my long clinical career, I have had opportunities at times to learn about locked units. I have worked in those units at all levels of security – low, medium and high. More recently, I was involved in some independent reviews of people with intellectual disabilities who were being detained and segregated in locked units. It is possible to understand how people who are very distressed and who may hurt other people, end up in very restricted environments. But it does not feel humane, and many people are working towards a better approach. My position is that, if we meet the needs of distressed individuals, then the need for restrictive practices will disappear. The individuals who become patients in locked units usually have a long history of distress. A survey of the case notes will often reveal that they had periods of being more settled and then, after about two years, the behavioural problems returned.

Putting this into the context of emotional development, it occurred to me that, what could be happening is that, upon moving into a new environment with elements of trust, they begin to make some progress in their emotional development. As a result, the people providing their support start to relax, thinking that they are much improved, and reduce the level of support they provide, which in turn removes the emotional security and the distressed behaviour returns. If this is what is happening, then it needs to be addressed. It was common practice at one time to offer two-year placements for treatment and this has proved to be unworkable. Some people become distressed at the end of the two years because they can't envisage what follows next. Some others become distressed by the withdrawal of support and talk of independence. Some need five or ten years of therapeutic support, and short-term placements will never be effective.

One of the noticeable aspects of this type of support, to me, is the way that people will engage in very destructive behaviour leading to restraint, which seems to be a maladaptive way of securing physical contact. I remember a situation many years ago when I was called out in the night to a young woman in restraint. When I got there, she was being held by five people, four of whom were men. She was screaming and crying and struggling. When I got there, she calmed down and started to tell me about what was causing her distress. Usually, that information would be shared within the confidentiality of a therapy session, not in front of five members of staff. However, the information was so distressing for her, and thinking about it had clearly been what had upset her in the first place, so it seemed right to explore with her what she was saying, what it meant, and how the 'being held' was helping her. It became possible to reframe restraint as therapeutic holding, which she understood and experienced, and the staff began to understand and to be less angry with her.

In a situation like that, it becomes possible to address the horror of the early trauma because it's there in front of you. The restriction and loss of control, being overpowered by people stronger than yourself, will remind a person of their traumatic childhood. If we link this back to early trauma that has interfered with the ability to relate to others on an equal basis, then we can see how that inability has led to more misunderstanding and more trauma throughout life. The inability to hold onto a sense of self, because the sense of self is not fully formed, leads to being held in a restricted way because there is no formula for providing that support in a non-restrictive way. However, appropriate support is possible if it is thought through, planned and designed around the individual, and provided in a supportive living setting.

More recently I was consulted about a young woman who seemed to be, according to her staff, driving them to hold her in restraint. In studying the patterns of her behaviour and the feelings she was bringing out in the staff who supported her, it became clear that it was a similar situation. This young woman needed to be held because she couldn't emotionally hold herself and her identity. The underlying psychological drive was pushing her to push the staff to provide her with what she needed. Unfortunately, being in a hospital setting and the detention order under the Mental Health Act meant it was not seen as therapeutic holding. It was possible to secure a holding 'pod' for this young woman that made a cocoon for her to be held in, thus avoiding so much physical contact and restraint. She reacted well to the pod and was able to use it in the way that a small child would seek the cot or pram when the world gets too much for them.

It is known that there are a number of quite severely autistic young people in very restricted environments in the UK, but studies on this are not well-funded. The majority of them are young men who have become too strong and destructive to stay at home with their families. They escalate to segregated environments which can be a very lonely existence, but it suits their need to avoid confusing contact with people. These young men have never been able to develop fully interactive relationships with their families or anyone else, and they are emotionally very immature with emotional development measured at the practicing stage, which is ten to 15 months in neurotypical development. An 18-year-old, six-foot tall, young man with an emotional age of a one-year-old is going to find life extremely difficult. It is also extremely difficult for staff supporting them to relate to the discrepancy between what they can see physically and the person's arrested emotional state. There is also further de-synchrony with the cognitive ability as this is usually not as delayed as the emotional development. As a consequence, they can often plan mischievous activities and many ways of destroying the environment around them. They may also have cognitively come to the conclusion that their environment is hostile to them, prompting them to attack it constantly, breaking everything, and needing an environment that is very robust with punch-resistant walls, no pipework, recessed lighting, and almost bare.

It isn't hard to imagine emotionally young people, as described above, stuck at that infantile stage, with no knowledge of the world and no understanding of it or the people around them. If they do not make that initial connection to a caring adult, they continue to remain lost and cut off from others. Families and support staff can feel very rejected, even hated, because, to a large extent, they are irrelevant to the individual who is locked into a world of autism or anxiety, much of which they don't understand. Once the de-synchrony has been fully understood, for example, if someone is 18 years physically, perhaps six years cognitively, but only one year emotionally, it can be more clearly accepted that they will be distressed and confused. If the appropriate emotional environment is then put in place, it becomes possible to activate the cognitive skills to work together on supportive relationships and appropriate activities. The use of the pod as described above, or a safe room, can provide the equivalent of a cot or pram for cooling down. With a neurotypical child who has become confused and distressed, crying and lashing out, it is usual practice to hold them if that's what they need, or to let them calm down alone.

It has been my experience that, when I explain the meaning of a person's distressed behaviour to a family or staff group, there is a fairly immediate relaxation and reduction in anxiety. Having a model of understanding helps enormously.

If we seek to reduce the use of restricted environments, and the excessive use of calming medication, we need to have a model of understanding the behaviour that we see, the meaning of that behaviour and approaches that address the person's emotional needs. This approach clearly needs to be benevolent, caring and fun. It is possible to design such environments and support plans that meet the person's needs. However, they are still not widely available, and people find themselves in assessment and treatment units or long-stay residential placements with very restricted lives. It is to be hoped that books like this, which describe alternatives, will become more readily accepted and available to commissioners and providers of services.

There will, of course, always be some people who have committed serious assaults on other people for reasons other than those described above. In my experience, I have never met a perpetrator who wasn't first a victim. However, it does seem that some people have been so damaged by their experiences of abuse that they continue to lash out at other people. There is perhaps a distinction here between people who are more severely intellectually disabled and those who are less so. People who are verbal and more cognitively able can engage in therapy to address their trauma and make positive choices to behave differently, if their trauma can be resolved. People who are more severely disabled may be more dependent on what is provided for them and their reactions on an emotional level. Given the right support, they should be able to make some progress towards not needing to hurt others.

There are times when it looks like the right intervention can be provided, but then it is taken away for financial reasons, indicating a lack of understanding of the possible progress that can be made. In the days of the old long-stay hospitals, people were kept together in relatively large groups in restricted environments. Community care set out to stop this, but sadly new institutions are developing with the same problems as the old ones.

We end up with a 'warehousing' model whereby people are kept and fed. They have a safe place to be but do not make progress to a better quality of life. It is hoped that more people in positions of power will recognise the possibilities that come from understanding the impact of trauma on the development of self, and provide more early interventions. If all young people who have arrested emotional development were recognised earlier, it must be possible to provide a therapeutic intervention and avoid the repeated trauma and deepening distress that follows.

Chapter 23: Extending our thinking to emotionally unstable 'Personality Disorder'

The more study I have made of the impact of trauma and the emotional developmental model, the more relevant I have found it to be. Initially, the work began with people with intellectual disabilities, and that has been the area of focus for most publications. The emphasis on this group came, for me, from my experience of knowing many people with intellectual disabilities who were showing distress. Another important factor was the persistence of the distress, regardless of the potential changes in their environment or care. That led me to think that the condition of emotional developmental delay may be permanent and not amenable to recovery. However, what has been shown over the years is that it is not a fixed condition and recovery is possible. That fact inevitably led me to question the impact of early trauma on people without intellectual disabilities. The next few chapters are going to address some of these issues, beginning with the condition previously known as borderline personality disorder and now called emotionally unstable personality disorder.

If we were to carry out the Frankish Assessment of the Impact of Trauma (FAIT) with someone with the diagnosis of EUPD and without intellectual disabilities, what we would invariably find is that they are stuck at the early rapprochement stage of development – not fully formed into a stable personality. If we consider the associated behaviours with the early rapprochement stage, then it becomes very obvious. At this stage of development in the neurotypical process, the young child would be demanding, exploring, into everything, continually questioning and not settling unless in the presence of a stable and reliable adult. If we consider that anyone who suffers a traumatic life event at that stage of their ordinary development may suffer an arresting of that development, then we can see the logic of the process. It begins to look like common sense, although that is clearly not how it is seen. If we did begin to look at this client group in this way, we might find it easier to provide them with the input they need and with sufficient support to enable them to develop further and establish a more secure sense of self. At the moment, the usual approach is to provide medication for the person's anxiety and erratic behaviour. People with emotionally unstable personality disorder are frequently angry and disruptive, often causing distress to themselves, their families, their friends and members of the public. In my own clinical experience, I have met many people with this diagnosis and most of them are significantly distressed. They are unable to understand or accept the constant rejection they experience from people who expect them to behave like adults when inside there is still a traumatised child.

If we accept the process that has led to the difficult behaviour then we can begin to think about ways to help individuals to grow into a more stable personality, and lead more settled and less traumatic lives. If we go back again to the requirements for trauma informed care, we come immediately to the need for the availability of a significant other to maintain emotional stability in an emotionally nurturing environment. While this can be accepted for people with intellectual disabilities, it is less available for neurotypical people with emotional difficulties. There are residential care facilities for this client group, and many hospital beds are taken up by people with the condition when their distress has led them to self-harm or cause a disturbance to others. But there is usually a limited staffing level and a lack of understanding of the need for a specific named individual to be available at all times. Some people can manage with regular therapeutic input, perhaps on a weekly basis, and can manage in between sessions to hold themselves together. If the therapy provided follows the attachment-based model that John Bowlby prescribed, there is a real possibility of significant improvement. People of average or above average intellect can usually grasp the information that they've been given about their condition and, after a period of processing, can come to a position where they can help themselves and their emotional development. Some may be very angry at first, and especially angry at the people who were looking after them when they were young. It won't be a surprise to know that many of the people I have worked with were adopted as toddlers. It is a difficult decision to make when a toddler needs a new home because they cannot stay with their birth parents. Many adoptions are successful, of course, but there are a significant number who do not process the trauma of their early life, mainly because they were non-verbal at that time and couldn't tell anybody. Others have been traumatised by family breakups, the arrival of siblings, environments that are not geared up for child rearing and so on. There is no doubt that childhood is a very risky time and it is a miracle that more people are not distressed.

We need to consider again the issue of the difference between intellectual/cognitive development and emotional development. There is still an emphasis in infant mental health on social development, but this does not always capture that pre-social stage that is covered by the assessment of the impact of trauma. It does seem to be perhaps too painful for people to accept that babies and toddlers can be so severely affected by their life experiences. If we can get to a position of shifting that understanding to a deeper recognition of the meaning of early relationships, then many people benefit. Winnicott's book The Child, the Family and the Outside World, written in the middle of the last century, spells it out perfectly and it would be of benefit to anyone who studied his work. He fell out of favour when he indicated that autism may be a response to emotional difficulties in the mother-child relationship. The work of emotional development being reported here would support the possibility that this is the case. However, it is my contention that it is more than the mother-child relationship that affects emotional development. I will discuss autism in a further chapter, but it is sufficient to mention here that we don't know, and can't be sure, of the cause and effect relationship in a number of conditions. What we do know is that if we see infantile behaviour in an adult, we can be fairly confident that it reflects some traumatic experience at the relevant stage of development. The important thing to remember is that, once it is identified, there are approaches that help. There is further importance in recognising that it is a developmental glitch rather than an illness, and this, for some people, is very reassuring. For others, it is very frightening, as they have gained some comfort from the use of medication and sometimes enough support.

Emotionally unstable personality disorder is a long title for a condition that is distressing for the individual and for their friends and family. It may be more helpful to think of it in a more simplified way, and this may lead to early identification of the person's difficulties. If the early developmental trauma was recognised in childhood and the appropriate interventions took place, there is every possibility of a significant reduction in adult referrals. And, more importantly, a significant improvement in the quality of life of the individuals concerned. What I would like to see, in time, is early intervention when the difficulties are first noted, which will often be in the first two years of schooling, but hopefully before that.

I am aware that what I have said in this chapter is probably contentious. However, it feels important to say it when I reflect on the number of people with the condition of EU PD who have benefited from this understanding. I also reflect on the many people with the condition who continue to bounce around the system as revolving-door patients, in and out of hospital, in and out of medication changes, often with associated suicide attempts or criminal damage, all of which can be seen as a cry for help. Sadly, because this cry for help persists long after professionals believe they have offered their help, individuals are perceived to be ungrateful and not worthy of further input. If we could get to a stage of fully understanding the emotional pain that these individuals experience, it may be more likely that they would receive, or more of them would receive, what they need. Again, my ideal position, is that the difficulties are identified much earlier and that individuals are provided with the right emotional support to enable them to develop a much more secure sense of self.

Chapter 24: Prevention

If we start early, we can make a difference.

Most of what we've been talking about so far has been about how to intervene to make things better when early trauma is identified at a later stage in life. I want to think now about what we could do to recognise when someone has been traumatised more recently, and do something at the time. One of the big issues with children with different needs is that any interruption in their development can be seen as part of the original condition. As a consequence, their reaction to a life event may either go unnoticed or be labelled as something different.

If we want to avoid distress, huge interventions and possible detention, then we need to be alert to the early signs of arrested emotional development in response to trauma. To do this, we will need to be aware of the indications of straightforward development, in order to recognise if there has been an interruption.

When we assess the impact of trauma at later life stages, we don't assess for the first and sixth stages of development, mainly because they would not be likely to occur. The first stage, symbiosis, belongs to the very first few weeks of life and it is rare to find an older child or adult still stuck at this stage. But it is not impossible and, if someone has dropped into a semi-catatonic state, then they will need an intervention based on the ideas of symbiosis. If we are looking at children traversing the symbiotic stage successfully, we will link into the well-known recommendation of skin-to-skin contact between mother and newborn child. This is the symbiotic stage where mother and baby are still almost connected as one body. Some babies seem to be very fractious from the beginning and the implication of this trauma approach is that they may have found the birth process to be traumatic. If we use that as a basis for thinking of intervention, we would seek to help mother and baby to form a strong symbiotic relationship in the hope that this would facilitate positive development. There are also some babies who don't seem to cry, and although this can be seen as a positive, it may be more appropriate to see it as a shutdown state that needs to be addressed, again, by establishing a strong symbiotic relationship. Most new mothers, particularly with their first child, will rely on neonatal staff and families to advise them. It would probably be useful for all expectant parents to know the emotional developmental model and its natural progression. It must be advantageous to recognise the stages of development and to work towards enabling the baby to pass through them seamlessly and painlessly.

Within a few weeks and through the early months there will be the development of differentiation behaviours, as the baby begins to be more alert and take note of the environment and its own body. We notice that they begin to look at their fingers and toes or the people who look at them where they are lying. If we don't see these behaviours, we need to first of all question why; has something happened to make this baby freeze and not interact? We need to ask questions about what can be done, and actively encouraging exploration of self and surroundings can be useful, while maintaining at all times the security of the parental relationship. The presence of the significant other is crucial and it may be that an absence of the significant other is the cause of the lack of differentiation behaviours. If the significant other is absent, that may be for unavoidable reasons like illness, postnatal depression, loss of a parent or some other stressful life event. If the expected significant other is not available, then someone else needs to actively fulfil that role to ensure that emotional development continues. If there is a continued absence, then it is likely that there will be an arrest of the child's emotional development and consequent symptoms. A substitute significant other will probably have to go back to the symbiotic stage to establish a close trusting relationship before the natural process of development can restart. Again, this may need the support of neonatal staff to provide guidance and support. There is the risk that the child will sleep more in response to the trauma, leading everyone to feel relief, when in fact it may be that it's not a positive response. These ideas can be quite contentious, and it is extremely difficult to carry out research to establish the validity of these ideas. It would be unethical to deny children the presence of a significant other in order to test the theory. But if we look at the emotional development of, for example, the Romanian orphans who suffered so much under the rule of Caeuşescu in the 1980s, we can see the consequences of the absence of a significant other in early childhood.

We would expect the baby to begin to be more active towards the middle of the first year, rolling over and responding to the primary carer (the significant other). We would also expect that there would be more behaviours evident in the presence of the significant other than in the presence of other people. This is healthy development and to be encouraged. If this doesn't begin to happen for a child with another disability, then that can again be assumed to be part of the disability. This needs to be tested out by encouraging activity with lots of smiles and positive encouragement. It needs to be remembered that this is not about skill acquisition to prove ability, but is about emotional development and being comfortable with their self and their relationship with their primary carer.

If there is a known dramatic event in this stage, for example the possible reaction of the parents to the news that the child has a disability, then they will potentially need extra support to be able to continue to provide the emotional support that the child needs in order to progress through the practicing stage. As this stage involves lots of repetitive behaviours, it is strongly associated with autism. It is not known what impact delayed or arrested emotional development has on the development of autism, but it seems to me that it is likely to be connected. If by this time it is known that the child has a disability and will have a developmental delay, perhaps in physical as well as cognitive development, then there tends to be an emphasis on physical skill acquisition, sometimes at the expense of recognising the child's emotional needs. It is vital that the child is encouraged to be with their significant other and to practice any skills they have. This of course includes things like smacking mum in the face, pulling her hair, pulling her glasses off and so on. These are normal behaviours for the practicing stage, but may carry on for longer times with a child with a disability. It is important to recognise that the child would not be engaging in these behaviours unless they felt comfortable and acceptable to those people present. In the event, if it is noticed that there is a delay in the progression to practicing, or if the child has to move to the care of other people, it may be necessary to establish the closeness of the differentiation stage in the relationship, before expecting more practicing behaviours.

It becomes important to notice when early rapprochement behaviours begin. If it is missed, the child can start to withdraw in a traumatised state. In neurotypical development, early rapprochement begins with the ability to say no and the ability to walk away. These are both behaviours that challenge the primary carer and begin the process of two-way interaction. A child with a disability who cannot walk away will struggle with this stage. A child with a cognitive impairment who doesn't speak can't say no. It becomes vital for the adults involved to be alert to whatever the child can do to assert themselves. This may of course be seen as maladaptive behaviour if it takes the form of self-harm, screaming, or some other behaviour that is hard to tolerate. However, if an interruption in emotional development is recognised at this stage, or a known traumatic event has happened, then intensive interaction approaches can help. If this can include healthy eye contact, physical contact, low expressed emotion and warmth, it can be possible to establish the early rapprochement stage.

Again, if you are faced with the situation of somebody who had shown solid rapprochement behaviours that have now stopped, it is important to re-establish the practicing stage and gently encourage a return to early rapprochement. If any sign of irritation or disappointment in the apparent lack of development is shown, then the child will respond negatively. At this stage, there will be an awareness of the parental emotional commitment and that can lead to further withdrawal by the child if it is not enough. If the trauma is recognised and the child is helped to process it and move on, then there is every possibility that the hiccup in development can be overcome.

The early rapprochement stage is quite long and quite challenging in neurotypical development. It's also quite fun as there is lots of development, interest in the world, and the obvious development of the child as a separate personality. This, of course, leads to clashes of will and the parent must guide the child gently side-by-side with them and avoiding confrontation. It is during this stage that, quite often, a sibling arrives, which can be challenging. This can be even more challenging if the older child has a disability and is known to be different, and the new baby does not have a disability. This can create enormous challenges for the parents, and they need support to be able to meet the emotional needs of the disabled child as well as the new arrival. Parents need a lot of support at this time to ensure that all needs are met as far as possible. If there are immediate signs of regression in the older child then it is important to re-establish the level of support that was provided at the practicing stage, gently encouraging a return to the previous level of development. This does require that the parents, or another significant other, are able to be generous in their tolerance of a return to more infantile behaviour, knowing that it cannot or is unlikely to last for long, so long as the need is addressed.

The late rapprochement stage, equivalent to the three to four-year-old child in neurotypical development, may not be reached by a child with a disability. However, there is a lot of evidence that many people do, and many progress emotionally to a higher level than they do cognitively. However, trauma at this stage can be quite devastating as the child has already begun to have strong and trusting relationships which, if severed, will have a dramatic effect. The signs of trauma at this stage would be regression, possibly including toilet and food behaviours. It is vitally important that the regression is recognised as a traumatic reaction to something emotional, and that the emotional need is met with understanding and compassion. If the child is not able to say what has happened, and no one notices what happened, then it is important to try and find out. Drawing sometimes helps a young child to show what has distressed them. It is important to recognise how idiosyncratic trauma is, and that what is traumatic for one person may not be traumatic for another. If the difficulty is not addressed at this stage, it will go on to be an issue until it is addressed. When we reflect on the individuals that we know, often in secure accommodation, with really difficult rapprochement behaviours, we can see how important it is to work through those difficulties when the child is small. Having your hair pulled by a little child is very different from having it pulled by an 18-year-old who's bigger than you.

Ideally, all people with disabilities would have sufficient emotional support to be able to reach a stage of self-knowledge and acceptance that allows them to function well enough in the world. Sadly, we know that this is not the case. We also know that families do not get enough support when children first shows symptoms. It is hoped that by sharing some of these thoughts and ideas we will eventually get to a stage where all neonatal and childcare staff recognise the signs and can help families at an earlier stage.

Chapter 25: Wider implications for non-intellectually disabled children

All of my work has been directed and influenced by people with intellectual disabilities. However, it has become clear to me as time has gone on, that people without intellectual disabilities can also suffer from early trauma. There is a chapter in this book on why we aren't all traumatised and there may be some overlap here, but it felt important to draw some similarities and differences into focus.

When we consider the trajectory from biological birth to psychological birth, we can see the complexity of the processes involved, and it is something of a miracle that most of us pass through the stages without incident. But we all know of children who have struggled to go to school when it's time. Some of them will have rejected nursery and playgroup and that has been accepted as their choice. But school is not voluntary, it's part of the statutory requirement that we attend school, usually from the age of five, although many children start school before they are five, going into a reception class where it is hoped that their social development will equip them for learning. There is an opportunity in reception for them to develop relationships with other children and adults who are not their parents. If we go back to Donald Winnicott's book *The Child, the Family and the Outside World*, we are clearly looking at the 'outside world stage' when it comes to beginning school life. It is, of course, desirable that all children are comfortable in their own identity before they need to go to school.

Children with disabilities may be eligible for support from the beginning of their lives, and families will have a range of support staff to help them. This includes physiotherapy, occupational therapy, speech therapy, maybe a Portage scheme and other specialist provision. If they are showing signs of emotional difficulties, or emotional developmental delay, they are likely to be identified at an early stage. Their difficulties may not be labelled correctly, because of the emphasis on cognitive rather than emotional development, but they will usually be identified as children with additional needs. This may lead to an education health care plan (EHCP) before they go to school. They are less likely to be missed, although, again, perhaps the difficulty is not correctly identified. If the difficulty does lead to the allocation of one-to-one support, then the provision of the significant other, even if it's not understood, may be provided.

Children without disabilities will not usually have come to the attention of anyone before attending school. The only healthcare they are likely to have received will be from the general practitioner for nothing more than vaccinations and short-term infections. Attending school may be a shock, and will be especially so for children who have emotional developmental delays. If they do have an issue, it may be difficult to identify the source of the difficulty. It is often at this stage that parents ask for an assessment by the educational psychologist, looking for identification of the difficulty and guidance on what to do. The emphasis is always on learning, which is appropriate for education, but may miss the subtle identification of the delayed sense of self, which can impact the child's identity and confidence to engage in the opportunities which are provided by an educational environment.

If we could get to a position where all children received an assessment of their emotional development through the stages, which would include more general information for parents, nurseries and nursery school staff, we could hopefully reach a point where early intervention prevented the development of further problems, and facilitated good interaction with education and, consequently, better outcomes. There is, necessarily, a need for children to work together as a group in the classroom. This is required for the benefit of all in the education environment. The child who cannot function in a group situation is therefore severely disadvantaged. It can of course be helpful to provide additional support with a teaching assistant, but this does need to be focused. There is always a risk of maintaining the status quo, rather than facilitating development. I studied at one time for a postgraduate certificate of education (PGCE) and did my teaching practice in three different schools. It was a requirement, although the course was for teaching children with severe intellectual disabilities, that we do one placement in an ordinary mainstream school. As I was inclined already at that stage to the special needs of children, I was struck by the youngsters who could not function in classroom situations. However, I was not popular for pointing out that a particular child could not transfer information from the blackboard to the paper. When I pointed out to the teacher that this particular child was not able to relate to "the outside world" and so could not benefit from class teaching without additional support, it was not accepted in the terms which I saw it. The child was considered to be uncooperative and unprepared for school by his parents. There must be many children like him in reception classes and further up the chain in primary schools. This is such an important life stage for children and the identification of difficulties saves an enormous amount of intervention at a later stage.

I have a vision of all children having a 40-minute assessment of their emotional developmental stage. This could be administered at ages one, two and three, ideally, with interventions put in place if delays are identified. The evidence is growing that once the situation is identified and an appropriate support package is put in place, there is quite a rapid improvement. The evidence also shows that no intervention equals no change. What I am suggesting may be quite radical, and I reflect on the reception that Donald Winnicott received when he was saying similar things. My argument is that the very complex issues that he talked about can be simplified into a model that can be used by everyone. Particularly if it is used in a preventative way, to avoid further difficulties. For example, if somebody is stuck at the practising stage and is helped, then in six months is able to move to rapprochement, their lives will be significantly changed and helped forever. If they're not identified, and stick at the practising stage forever, they will struggle through life even if they are cognitively not impaired. The likelihood of the development of some other disorders is significantly increased. If at the practising level, then we are looking at conditions like obsessive-compulsive disorder, autism spectrum disorders, and probably bipolar disorders. Some serious personality disorders would be identified as well. It would take a massive research programme to gather the evidence to say that this is exactly right, and that will be covered in the final chapter of this book.

All of these issues must be seen to be supportive and not critical. As has been stated elsewhere, trauma is idiosyncratic and we cannot predict who will react to what, and how they will react. None of us are immune and there is no need to be ashamed or critical of parents if a child becomes arrested in their emotional development. It's something that happens, and the positive thing is that, if we recognise when it has happened, we can do something about it.

Chapter 26: Why aren't we all traumatised?

A few reflections on the human condition.

The more I think about the level of trauma that exists in the people that I work with, the more I question the role of trauma in all of our lives. And we do of course all have traumatic experiences, and some of those will have happened before we individuated. It seems to me that the main issue we need to consider is vulnerability to the negative consequences of traumatic experiences.

When we consider the work of psychoanalysts, psychotherapists and hypnotherapists, we are looking at ways of exploring the impact of past events on the present. There must be a factor, or factors, that influence the impact and reaction to life events. And it must also be recognised that many life events facilitate growth in the personality, so not all consequences are negative.

Freud was the first person to publish his thoughts about the unconscious, and it seems to me that the unconscious is very much about the early life experiences that shape who we become. Carl Jung and Melanie Klein developed these ideas, with Klein being perhaps the first person to look at very early life experiences, even going so far as life before birth. If we consider, now, the possible impact of traumatic pregnancies and traumatic births from the model put forward in this book, we can see how useful it is to consider the possibility of a longer-term impact. This is not to frighten us, but more to reassure us that, if we consider seriously what the impact of trauma may be, we can offer help and support to ameliorate that impact.

If we go on to consider the work of Donald Winnicott and John Bowlby in particular, we get more into the study of early childhood. Freud is known to have said that the age of seven was critical, but others have gone on to look at earlier stages of development, and my own work is taking me into the critical period of the first three to four years. There is no doubt in my mind that the description of childhood that Winnicott put forward in *The*

Child, the Family and the Outside World captures what really happens. But it does seem that Western society was not ready to accept what Winnicott was saying, and perhaps some of this is because it is perceived to be criticism of parents. My position on parents is that even the most well-meaning parents have no parental training before becoming parents, and few have access to specific support. I argue strongly for more training of neonatal and paediatric staff. There is a huge issue of resilience in those staff and parents as we all carry our own specific life experiences that make us who we are.

John Bowlby's work on attachment is also very significant and now widely respected. Others have gone on to produce measurement tools for different types of attachment. These are useful, although they do seem to me to indicate a fixed state that has to be worked with, and do not give much positive enthusiasm for recovery from a fixed state. This can, of course, be useful to discover what the state is at which a particular person is stuck and what accommodations can be put in place. However, in my experience, it is more likely that it will be given as a fact that the child has a disorganised attachment style if that is what is found, without necessarily producing a way of working with the child that might help them to recover.

It is within the context of these theories that I was working when I found Mahler's work. I should mention here that she worked with her colleagues Pine and Bergman, not alone, and she was working with a whole range of children, not necessarily ones who were atypical in their development. Although I have taken the work into the world of intellectual disability, because that's where I found it to be very useful, I am left now with the question mark over what happens to all of us in neurotypical development. It might help to spend a few minutes reflecting on how you, the reader, differ from everybody else that you know, including your immediate family. There is often speculation about why one child within a family is different from the rest. There is often confusion about the specific differences as it seems strange that children growing up in the same family could be so different. If we consider that anything can be traumatic for any child at any time, it becomes more obvious that no two people will be the same. The first child in the family has the traumatic experience of being nurtured by parents who have no previous experience. They also have the trauma of further children arriving if they are one of a sibling group. Apart from these major obvious difficulties that could be traumatic, there is the full range of real-life experiences that can be interpreted by an individual child as traumatic. I think of incidents like a toddler getting separated from their parent in the supermarket or the beach, and experiencing the absolute terror of those moments until they are found. We all have events like that in our history and these events all shape who we have become. If we have been very frightened as a child, we may become wary and withdrawn, or angry and possibly aggressive. If we have experienced the arrival of other children, we may have become less confident, or more withdrawn, or more openly friendly, or any of a wide range of responses. Some of those responses will be prompted by our parents and other family members. Some of them will come from our own innate abilities and disabilities. If we consider the complexity of the human psyche, we can begin to respect the impact that events in the early stages of our lives might have.

One of the big issues that I want us to consider here is the impact of events in the pre-verbal period of development. There is no way that a pre-verbal child can tell us how they are feeling about what they are experiencing. They are totally dependent on adults to keep the world safe, to provide experiences for growth, facilitate processing of difficult things, and to be alert to anything untoward that may interfere with the positive progression to the next stage of childhood. It seems to be close to a miracle that any of us reach adulthood successfully! A deeper respect for those early years seems to be a requirement for good health and social services. The way in which childcare is provided, childminders and nurseries and creches, needs to be trauma informed from the beginning. All staff need to be trained to provide the level of emotional support that is required. Parents need to be provided with what is required if they are going to use alternative care for their infant. And most parents nowadays are put in the position of needing to use alternative care so that they can go to work. It can be successful, and be a growth experience for the child if their emotional needs are taken seriously. Unfortunately, some children who are traumatised in very early childhood are not ready to go to nursery when they need to. I am reminded of the 'handicapped children's centre' model that was around when I was young. And I remember visiting them in my early days after qualification as a psychologist, and being horrified by the distress that I saw and heard. There was an assumption that children with disabilities would be better off in alternative care from a much younger age than was accepted for children without disabilities. We now know that this is completely opposite to what is required as children with disabilities would be more likely to have an emotional developmental delay as well as cognitive impairment.

With the requirement for both parents to continue working has come the development of more childminding and nurseries. Many of the people who are providing these services are doing a very good job, but may not have the expertise to recognise a traumatised infant or to know what to do if they see one. There is a strong argument for discrimination over the starting age for a particular child to go to alternative care. However, if the significant other model is in place for the early days with no glitches, there is every possibility that even a traumatised child can cope. It is vital that the parent passes the child to a trusted other's hands and that the trusted other is able to fulfil that role until such time as the child is handed back to the parent. Many parents are in the position of needing their child to be collected from nursery by grandparents. It follows from this that the grandparents also need to understand their role as significant others. Most grandparents do understand this and will do their best to keep the world safe for their grandchildren. But there is no doubt that both parents, grandparents and nurseries or childminders will struggle with a child who is not conforming to expectations. And usually, they will not know why the child is fractious or withdrawn until the child is old enough to talk. Even then the child won't necessarily be able to explain.

Taking into consideration all the hazards we have to endure in our early childhood, it becomes obvious that the events that happen in any individual child's life shape who that individual becomes. This explains why we are all different. We all respond in an idiosyncratic way to the life experiences that we have. I wonder if it might be helpful for you, the reader, to reflect on your own early life experiences, those that you know about, bearing in mind few of us can remember our very early childhood. Our earliest memory is usually associated with something traumatic for us at the time. One of the key questions in a psychotherapy assessment is to ask about the earliest memory. Not many people can recall anything before the age of three, although some can. It does seem that the stage of individuation is associated with some sort of crisis, and that is described in this book. The psychological birth moment is described as either a shrug of acceptance or an explosion of feelings in a tantrum followed by acceptance of self as separate. If we reflect on the people that we know, and on our psyche, we can perhaps get in touch with our own significant events that made us who we are, including those from very early childhood that we may have been told about rather than remember.

We can look at all the major mental illnesses and personality disorders from the position of the emotional developmental model. There has been a lot of research over the years into genetic and environmental influences on the development of major disorders. There has been resistance to looking more extensively at the psychoanalytic model, possibly because treatment is so long and expensive. But if we can accept the theoretical position put forward in this book, and apply it more widely to specific groups referred to in the previous chapters, we could come to a wider understanding of an infant's needs in early childhood for a secure emotional environment. If we couple this with early interventions to prevent the development of major problems, we could see a significant reduction in distress and illness.

In summary, to answer the question in the title of this chapter "Why aren't we all traumatised?", we realise that, in fact, we are all traumatised to some extent, and this is what makes us all unique. Our reaction to life events can make us more resilient, usually if they happen to us in the context of a secure emotional environment. Some of the traumatic life events lead to further psychological issues in later childhood and adulthood. If we are fortunate, there will be a good balance between things that help us to be resilient and things that make it more difficult.

Chapter 27: Further research

What can we do to explore the ideas developed in the preceding chapters?

Clearly, much of what I have said throughout this book is based on my own personal experience of many years of working with people who have emotional issues. In the early stages of my career, the only option for people with emotional difficulties was individual therapy or medication. For people with intellectual disabilities, there was very little availability of individual therapy. Most service provision and support was in the form of medication and various levels of residential care. I've talked about the old long-stay hospitals and the various movements that have progressed over the years to the model of care that we have now, which is primarily supported living rather than restricted environments, although there are still some, and some of these have made the news over the past few years with serious concerns about the level of oppressive treatment that has been provided. When I reflect on the scandals that led to the closure of the long-stay hospitals, I am saddened to recognise the same symptoms in the smaller establishments that are now provided.

People with intellectual disabilities are very vulnerable, and parents struggle with decisions about what sort of care they should have. This usually begins with concerns about appropriate education. Most parents have some concerns about the long-term opportunities there will be for their children. There is no doubt in my mind that the people who can't stay with their families, who escalate to secure care, are the ones who have additional emotional difficulties. Many people with intellectual disabilities live ordinary lives with their families, or move into semi-independent living, perhaps securing jobs and leading ordinary lives. We would like this for everyone. We do need to think about how to provide much earlier interventions if we are going to facilitate an improvement in the quality of life of everyone with an intellectual disability.

If we look at the wider context of people with emotional disabilities, with or without cognitive impairment, we need to consider the people who resort to physical violence and end up in prison, the people who have severe mental health difficulties and end up in psychiatric facilities, sometimes for years or for life. This is replicating the model of the long-stay hospitals that became a sort of human warehouse for people who could not cope with society.

If we consider that the human species is quite vulnerable, although notable for being more intelligent than other species, we can begin to think about what we can do to make it better. Huge research programmes are going on across the world, and some of them are relevant to what we are discussing here. However, it does not seem that the funding arrangements and the academic institutions are showing a particular interest in emotional disability or emotional development. There are studies of child development looking at cognitive development and physical development. What would be very good to see would be a long-term study from birth to age five, replicating the study by Margaret Mahler and her colleagues, adding the brain scans and other physical tests that would show change over time. There is a difficulty in having a control group in a study of intervention when difficulties are found, because it's unethical to deny the intervention to a control group. It must be possible, however, to follow a whole cohort for five years, intervening with any child that is shown to be demonstrating emotional developmental delay, and then checking the data against another geographical area where it was not possible to put in interventions. This would be an incidental or collective control group and, as there is no likelihood that the whole country would be provided with what's needed in one exercise, then the ethical consideration would become less of an issue. There have been, over the years, some two-town studies and one of those would be really useful. They are expensive but so is the restrictive 'care' that is provided for people who are stuck in their emotional development and continue to behave at the stuck stage of an infant.

Ideally, a study would follow a whole cohort, not just the ones who were identified as having known difficulties like a chromosome disorder, birth injury or other impairment. It may be difficult to get cooperation from parents for such a study, but it would certainly be worth trying. It is, of course, essential that an appropriate intervention and support package can be put in place when difficulties are identified. However, it is quite likely that many parents will be able to carry out the intervention themselves, once they understand the issues involved. Many parents recognise when their child is struggling in some way, although this may be more difficult with a first child or an only child where there is no comparison to be made. Raising children is not easy, and none of us are trained and prepared before they arrive. But it can and should be a joyful time to enable the baby to grow into a child, and the child to grow into an adult. And, of course, the second stage of growing into an adult through the teenage years can be extremely stressful, especially if the child has an emotional developmental disability.

This book is a collection of stories of real people living real lives who have benefited from the identification of their emotional disability and appropriate intervention. Most of those assessments and interventions have been relatively inexpensive. Ones that have been expensive have been in situations where the individual has suffered extreme trauma in early childhood which has gone unrecognised. The traumatic event itself may have been recognised, but not the emotional disability that has followed. Preventative work must be a better option for the individuals, support services, and for taxpayers who inevitably have to fund long-term care for people who can't care for themselves. There are some tragic stories of people with and without intellectual disabilities but with serious trauma in their first few years of life. I think particularly of children taken into care very young, adopted, again quite young, by adoptive parents who don't understand their child's inability to respond emotionally because of their traumatic experiences. There is a need for wider education programmes for adoptive parents, childcare staff, social workers involved in decision-making and the various courts that get involved with adoption or protection.

Ideally, a research study would identify a full cohort from a period of a year and follow all children born in that year in that area, putting in place assessments and appropriate interventions. It must be possible to do it, and I am hoping that someone who reads this will endeavour to make it happen. I am coming to the end of my career, and sadly it will not be something I can do myself.

Chapter 28: Summary

I want to begin this summary by reflecting on the usefulness of the model of developmental delay that has been outlined in this book. I've been using it for over 30 years now and have found it extremely useful, particularly in challenging the term 'challenging behaviour'. To me, we are looking at distressed behaviour. I know it was originally called challenging behaviour because of the challenges it presented to services, but over time it seems to have developed into being almost as pejorative as the old long-stay hospitals, which used to refer to behaviour wards. I reflect again on the use of the term and my own reaction to it. I would sincerely like the term 'emotional disability' to become more widely used. I would also like it to be more widely understood that all behaviour has meaning.

The initial motivation for this work came from the bringing together of my academic psychological knowledge, my long-stay hospital experience, and my introduction to psychodynamic psychotherapy. It became very obvious to me very quickly that psychodynamic psychotherapy can never be made available to all the people who need it. It was also clear to me that the efficacy of psychodynamic psychotherapy for people with intellectual disabilities was not widely recognised. I'm pleased to say that has changed significantly over the last 30 years, but the availability and the funding for sufficient individual therapy is just not there.

The motivation has been to come up with a way of working that could become generic, available to all, and become a mainstream model of care for people with intellectual disabilities and other types of complex needs. A number of people have worked with similar aims and I think particularly about Anton Dosen in the Netherlands. His work has been picked up by Mark Hudson in the UK, and Alan Skelley, also in the UK, has done extensive work on the emotional needs of people with intellectual disabilities.

If we continue to work with an understanding of trauma informed care, we can reach a position where we recognise emotional developmental delay and put in place responses at a much earlier stage. It would make a significant change in a lot of people's lives. But, inevitably, the question of research and proven results comes up. I have made several attempts over my career to get support for a suitable research project. I applied for access to some of the data from the 'Born in Bradford' project, but it was declined. The difficulty comes from researching something that it would be unethical to deny to a control group. I think the only way to research and get an answer to the question of the validity and reliability of the model would be to introduce the way of working to the whole service, perhaps in a whole town or city, gather data, and see if there was a reduction over five, ten and 15 years in the incidence and prevalence of autism, ADHD, EUPD, and a wide range of neuro-atypical development. Ideally, everyone would be assessed using the FAIT or something similar that captures someone's emotional developmental stage and recognises the point of individuation. It may be sufficient for research purposes to assess for individuation and to offer intervention for any child who hasn't individuated by the age of four. But if a child is traumatised by the age of 18 months, it seems wrong to wait until they are four to identify the difficulty. It is an ethical nightmare, and this may explain why such research has not been carried out so far.

What we do have here are the real-life stories of real-life people who have been offered an appropriate intervention when they have been referred with emotional difficulties. There is a wide range of stories in the preceding chapters, enabling us to see the wider implications of the model of trauma informed care. All of the people described in the preceding chapters have benefited from an understanding of their difficulties. They have not recovered from their primary condition, if they have a disability. The ones with a diagnosis of autism have not recovered from being autistic, but they have recovered from the consequences of the distress of the trauma and have been able to lead a better life. To check the possibility of perhaps reducing the incidence of conditions like autism, it would be vital to assess all children, at least at one year and two years, as part of their infant development assessments. And maybe that is where we need to start, by adding another component to the standard child assessments carried out. I have mentioned before about the social development that is assessed, and expressed my concern that it is necessary to look at earlier stages of development. Social development doesn't happen until the child has trust in the significant other person in their life.

Not all children have the benefit of their actual parent or parents from birth through to adulthood. However, if the significance of the significant other is fully appreciated, it should be possible to facilitate emotional development to a good-enough level. Donald Winnicott made it very clear that nobody can care for a child the way a natural mother can, and he saw this as a biological response. But we know the pressures of modern life on new mothers can be extreme, and that not all mothers can be fully available to their children, to be the significant other for the years that really matter. With the knowledge we have, we can begin to think more clearly about what could be possible. In her book *Why Love Matters*, Sue Gerhart brings in a different way much of what I'm saying here. The neuroscience is there to show that the brain develops better if everything is in place emotionally. It would require a massive study, with brain imaging from birth, which may be not appropriate, to really check out the impact of this model of care on the development of the brain. But there have been some small studies, and it may be that more are possible if there is a will to fund the research. I'm coming towards the end of my career now, so I will have to leave that to other people to take forward.

It is important to hold onto the research of the psychoanalysts from the 20th century and to look at how their findings can be applied today. Winnicott, in his books *Home is Where We Start From*, and *Deprivation and Delinquency*, gave clear descriptions and insights into the impact of trauma and its consequences. This work was published many years ago and has not been superseded.

Another gem of Winnicott's was the reference to, and use of, transitional objects. These can be used by children to compensate for short absences of the significant other, if used wisely. We will all know a little child who holds onto a particular toy or blanket. I'm not sure we can fully understand the value of that relationship. This is something that needs to be more widely understood and accepted. It may at times be suitable even to teach and encourage the use of a transitional object if the child is to be separated from its parent or significant other for some time.

The most important message of this whole book is that treatment and intervention are possible and effective if we either identify trauma when it occurs and respond appropriately, or put in place an appropriate interventions when we recognise it.

References

Baumeister AA (ed) (1967) *Learning Abilities of the Mentally Retarded in Mental Retardation.*

Beail N (1998) Psychoanalytical psychotherapy with men with intellectual disabilities: a preliminary outcome study. *British Journal of Medical Psychology* **71** (1) 1-11.

Beail N, Frankish P and Skelly A (2021) *Trauma and Intellectual Disability*. Shoreham-by-Sea: Pavilion Publishing and Media.

Bicknell J (1983) The psychopathology of handicap. *British Journal of Medical Psychology* **56** 167-178.

Bowlby J (1988) *A Secure Base*. London: Routledge.

Clarke AM & Clark ADB (1965) *Mental Deficiency: The Changing Outlook*. London: Methuen & Co.

Emerson E, Beasley F, Offord G, Mansell (1992) J An evaluation of hospital-based specialized staffed housing for people with seriously challenging behaviours. *Journal of Intellectual Disability Research* **36** (4).

Felce D (1996) Quality of support for ordinary living. In: J Mansell & K Ericsson (Eds.) *Deinstitutionalization and Community Living: Intellectual disability services in Britain, Scandinavia and the USA* (pp. 117–133). London: Chapman and Hall.

Frankish P (1989) Meeting the needs of handicapped people: a psychodynamic approach. *Journal of mental deficiency research* **33** 407-414.

Frankish P (2013) Measuring the emotional development of adults with ID. *Advances in Mental Health and Intellectual Disabilities* **7** (5) 272-276.

Frankish P (2016) *Disability Psychotherapy*. London: Karnac.

Frankish P (2022) Frankish Assessment of the Impact of Trauma. Shoreham-by-Sea: Pavilion Publishing and Media.

Freud S (1895) *Studies in Hysteria*. London: Hogarth.

Gerhardt S (2004) *Why Love Matters*. London: Routledge.

Klein M (1922) *The Psycho-analysis of Children*. London: Vintage.

LaVigna GW, Willis TJ & Donnellan AM (1989) The role of positive programming in behavioral treatment. In: E Cipani (Ed.) *The Treatment of Severe Behavior Disorders: Behavior analysis approaches* (pp. 59–83). American Association on Mental Retardation.

Mahler M, Pine F & Bergman A (1979) *The Psychological Birth of the Human Infant*. New York: Basic.

Piaget J (1977) The role of action in the development of thinking. In: *Knowledge and Development* (pp.17–42). New York: Springer.

Sinason V (1992) *Mental Handicap and the Human Condition: New approaches from the Tavistock*. London: Free Association, 2010.

Skelly A (2021) Finding out about trauma in the lives of people with intellectual disabilities; and what to do about it. In: *Trauma and Intellectual Disability*. Shoreham-by-Sea: Pavilion Publishing and Media.

Winnicott DW (1973) *The Child, the Family and the Outside World*. Middlesex: Penguin.

Winnicott DW (1984) *Deprivation and Delinquency*. London: Routledge.

Winicott D (1990) *Home is Where We Start From*. Middlesex: Penguin.